OUTSIDE IN

THE GARDENS AND HOUSES
OF TICHENOR & THORP

M. BRIAN TICHENOR and RAUN THORP

with JUDITH NASATIR

Foreword by PILAR VILADAS

Photography by ROGER DAVIES

VENDOME

NEW YORK • LONDON

Foreword

PILAR VILADAS

IN THE WORLDS OF ARCHITECTURE AND DESIGN, IT'S HARD TO resist the lure of the label. Categorizing someone's body of work as "contemporary," "traditional," or "modernist" is a kind of shorthand that offers an easy way to locate it on the stylistic spectrum. But it leaves little room for nuance. What if the work doesn't fall into any such category? Or, even more vexing, what if it falls into all of them? What if the work takes its stylistic cues from a variety of sources—from the client's preferences or possessions to the surrounding landscape or geography—according to the specifics of the project itself?

PRECEDING PAGES LEFT: On a rise overlooking cascading gardens and an adjacent golf course, a loggia extends the living spaces into the exterior. **PRECEDING PAGES RIGHT:** In a house where shades of blue reflect the owners' preferred palette, an azure vase seems a perfect ornament. **ABOVE:** One of Brian's paintings influenced the narrative of color that flows through the New York residence of a longtime bi-coastal client.

Such is the case with the work of Tichenor & Thorp Architects, the multidisciplinary firm founded in Los Angeles in 1990 by the husband-and-wife team of M. Brian Tichenor and Raun Thorp. The firm is noted for substantial, luxurious houses that skillfully incorporate traditional architectural styles—from Mediterranean to Colonial to California Modern—as well as those that are strikingly contemporary, and for gardens that sensitively frame these houses. Tichenor & Thorp has also completed thoughtful restorations of residential and commercial buildings, like the landmark Capitol Records tower, by iconic California architects of the twentieth century—from Paul Revere Williams and Roland Coate to Harwell Hamilton Harris. What all these buildings—old or new—have in common is an elegant livability, a careful attention to the needs and wishes of the client, and a constant concern for the relationship between architecture and the landscape that is reinforced by the firm's expertise in landscape and garden design, a rarity among architects today. Raun calls this approach "eclectic contextualism. . . . We like too many things too much to do only one thing." Brian adds, "The polyglot styles we work in are reflective of things our clients are moved by. Our designs all work the same way, but in different idioms." This philosophy is not lost on the firm's clients, a good

number of whom keep coming back to commission additional projects or to renovate existing buildings.

For Brian and Raun, architecture is just one element of a broader aesthetic and cultural universe. "We're not stridently architects," Brian explains. "It's part of a much larger picture, a great armature to put other things on. My interest in gardens is one example. Raun will obsess about nuances of hardware, or we'll both dig deep into fabrics for a while." Given their backgrounds, it makes perfect sense. Both Brian and Raun were raised in Southern California by forward-thinking parents who encouraged their varied enthusiasms. At age three, Brian was making model cars by drawing them on paper and then cutting and folding them into three-dimensional objects; an architect friend of his father's was so impressed that he told Brian a job would be waiting for him when he was ready. Later, Brian's interest in drawing and graphic art was encouraged by an aunt who owned an advertising agency. "I started getting *Communication Arts* magazine when I was ten," he recalls.

His father encouraged him to learn cabinetmaking when he was twelve, and by age sixteen he was making cabinetry on commission and designing T-shirts for mountaineering stores. In college (UCLA, Humboldt State, and UC Santa Barbara), Brian studied painting and printmaking, and later, architectural history. From the painter David Storey, one of his art teachers, he learned "the contextualization of design language, and how lineage works," concepts that applied not only to painting but to architecture too. But it was the architectural historian David Gebhard who urged Brian to go to architecture school, something that "hadn't occurred to me," he says.

Raun's path to architecture was similar, although slightly less circuitous. She grew up drawing, making her own books, sewing and embroidering, and nurturing her obsession with dollhouses, a book on which she "checked out of the library repeatedly." She also studied piano and classical guitar, and "played a lot of chess." Raun's mother, who was an arts patron, "exposed us to a lot of culture," she says. "My dad would do things with us like working with chemistry sets or making a hot-air balloon." As she recounts, "I thought I'd go to art school, then be a mathematician. What I actually liked was physics, and the applicability of it. But the compelling thing about math is puzzle solving, and the clarity of it," a skill that would one day come in handy when trying to accommodate a house's complicated program in a limited amount of space.

Still, just like Brian, Raun did not go to college intending to be an architect. She chose to attend Bryn Mawr because of its academic rigor, calling it "the quintessential liberal arts college." And although her major was The Growth and Structure of Cities, she chose it because it allowed her to approach the subject from a variety of disciplines, like economics and art history. What did pique Raun's interest in architecture was a not-for-credit, introductory design studio, and she ultimately wrote her senior thesis on collegiate architecture, designing a dormitory along with it. After college, Raun spent two years in New York working for an architecture firm before deciding to get a master's degree at UCLA. It was there, in 1983, that she and Brian met, during the fall of their first year in the program. In the years before Tichenor & Thorp's founding, Brian worked for the architect Charles Moore, at several of his many firms, and he also established his expertise in landscape and garden design in a joint venture with the noted landscape designer Nancy Goslee Power.

Their eclectic histories have served Brian and Raun well. Although they often work with noted interior designers—among those featured in this book are Thomas M. Beeton, John Cottrell, and the late Joe Nye—their knowledge of proportion, materials, furniture, and fine and decorative arts allows them to create sophisticated, comfortable rooms. For one of Raun's siblings, she and Brian designed a large, modern New York apartment—with luxe materials and finishes, and storage elements that enhance the existing architecture—that is perfectly suited to a growing family. In another New York project, the architects transformed an awkwardly laid-out apartment in the West Village into a spacious, comfortable home for a writer-director, filled with furniture and objects that all have their own stories. For a large house in Jackson Hole, Wyoming, the modernist furnishings and contemporary Western ranch house architecture are balanced by witty vernacular accents like a collection of framed bandannas. A sprawling Provençal estate in Rancho Santa Fe afforded Brian and Raun the opportunity to work closely with the owners' collections of French antiques. A comfortable Newport Coast house for Raun's parents incorporates her mother's passion for blue-and-white ceramics, including a series of tile panels that were hand-painted by Brian.

And in all these houses, architecture and landscape are in constant conversation, with the interiors framing views of the outdoors, while gardens, courtyards, and open-air dining areas create outdoor complements to their indoor counterparts. "We consider the connection to the outside at a much earlier stage than most firms," Brian explains. "Our houses take advantage of the land they're on; you have to have as many garden experiences as possible."

This idea has been shaped in part by the ongoing project that is one of the architects' favorites: their own house in Los Angeles, a 1940 design by the great California Modernist Harwell Hamilton Harris. The house, which had undergone an insensitive renovation by a previous owner, gave them the chance to bring it back to Harris's original design and has served as a laboratory for their ideas about domestic architecture and its relationship to landscape. The four gardens that Harris incorporated, Japanese-style, into the architecture are what gives the modestly sized (2,300-square-foot) house its sense of expansiveness; the design embodies the postwar California notion of indoor/outdoor living. "There's a clarity of thought in this house," Brian notes, "and the lessons can be

Inspired by the azulejos that adorn so much Mediterranean architecture, a blue-and-white tile painted by Brian adds an extra flourish of flora to a garden wall.

brought to any style." Since the house sits on a lot that's only a third of an acre, "the real luxury is the outdoor space."

Brian and Raun are bringing these lessons to a variety of new projects, including a large house in Monterey County that will have LEED platinum status for its extreme energy efficiency. But other projects are on a much larger scale: a development in Marina del Rey that includes three hundred apartments, public spaces, and a promenade; the gardens for a trio of historically significant apartment buildings in Orange County; an eight-story tower in El Segundo for a comprehensive cancer clinic; and a thirteen-acre Culver City campus for a biotech company that involves both new construction and adaptive re-use. But even these projects benefit from the architects' experience with residential design. "The big projects started because the clients loved our approach of integrating the outside and the inside," Brian says. "We design a campus the same way we design houses, protecting the outdoor spaces. The buildings have an almost residential feeling in the way they engage the land."

These days, the majority of Tichenor & Thorp's residential projects are designed in a modern vocabulary—even for repeat clients whose previous houses were more traditional. "We wouldn't mind doing another traditional house," Brian says, "but it's a different time, and I'm glad we've never been stuck in one style. We'll get to explore all the nooks and crannies of Southern California Modernism. It's never boring."

Introduction

FOR US, ARCHITECTURE IS FUNDAMENTALLY ABOUT TRANSFOR-mation. That plants us firmly in the camp of the historical continuum, a place where the past cannot help but inform the present. We look to the traditions of building and employ historical precedents to develop forms, structures, and gardens that are both embedded with meaning and full of modern comforts. The thrill of seeing a glimmer of the original idea within a historic house and garden in Los Angeles, or envisioning a modern farmhouse in an expanse of endless landscape in Jackson Hole, Wyoming, or imagining the possible ways to infuse the joy of light and

PRECEDING PAGES LEFT: In Raun's office, an ebonized desk takes pride of place in front of a wall of custom cabinetry. **PRECEDING PAGES RIGHT:** Against a backdrop of Blossfeldt prints that nod to the firm's horticultural expertise, a desktop vignette comments on the pattern, palette, and scale of the surroundings. **TOP:** Our studio keeps the reference material neatly contained but close at hand. **ABOVE:** Our conference room opens onto a furnished roof garden with the Los Angeles skyline as its backdrop.

elements of the organic into Manhattan interiors with limited views—that's part of our daily life as architects. So is the challenge of determining where on the spectrum of design thinking such ideas fall and the complex, nuanced process of puzzling out what each should become. The ultimate reward is finding ways to materialize the fully developed idea into corporeal reality—that's almost like magic.

Philosophically, aesthetically, and editorially speaking, we are inclusivists. And not just in matters of culture, period, and style. We feel that the vision for each undertaking should never be ours alone. We work with each client to develop the specific design DNA that informs their property—a modernist, courtyard-oriented retreat for art collectors in a historic neighborhood in Palm Springs; a classic, antiques-filled, Provençal-inspired bastide amid acres of French-inflected gardens near San Diego; a historically informed Anglo-Gallic fusion for a family in Bel Air— weaving together the strands of their greater dreams with the specific elements that matter to them the most. We explore as many potentialities as possible, see what clues those options reveal, puzzle out the various ramifications, and edit them down to the essential combination. Sketching is so important for us because drawings illustrate what words may not make clear. A rendering communicates design intent directly and reveals how and why particular ideas or options will, or won't, work in their particular context. For these reasons, in this volume we have included drawings alongside the photos of finished projects.

Within these pages, we have also paired the tale of each of the nine featured homes with an essay on one of the key ideas that underpin our design philosophy and thread through all our work. Analytical thinking and the search for the meaning in each decision drives our design process, as each project benefits from both an intellectual anchor and the driving force of a narrative. To have a defining idea

of who, what, where, when, why, and how—to tell the story or "play the movie"—of every inch of a design, space by space, room by room, inside and out, from beginning to end, provides an incredibly strong armature on which to hang each design decision, whether for a Portuguese-Spanish-inflected contemporary quinta atop a hill overlooking the Pacific or for a Pasadena property where inspiration from the English Regency meets the historicity of the late twentieth century.

Whether restoring a historic structure, revisiting a house and/or a garden we first worked on years ago, or envisioning and constructing a unique, private world from the ground up and from the property lines in, we focus on creating, framing, and celebrating the views from the outside in and the inside out. We inevitably factor in a conception of time and the transformational role it plays in both architecture and garden design. A fully layered garden may take as long as two decades to mature; a beautifully lived-in house, rather less. Through that tenure of development, the corporeal effect of each decision remains at the forefront. How will the spaces feel? What will the light be like? How best can we compose and direct the different views? What will the effect of the gardens be on the interiors? How can we seamlessly integrate the interior and exterior of the property? And how will those relationships affect the comfort levels inside and out?

We want every residence we create to be far more than a box of a structure amid gardens with no mitigation of light or views. Whatever style or vernacular the house needs to be, we search for its best expression. But our primary aim is to maximize the experiential quality of the designed spaces, both interior and exterior. In that way, every detail is meant to evolve over time. Gardens are a living canvas. They change as a matter of course. Houses should do the same in ways that correspond to the phases of our lives. For architecture is transformation. And transformation is not static.

TOP: Raun's office extends to a furnished garden terrace framed by the skyline of the Wilshire corridor and the hills beyond. **ABOVE:** Raun and Brian on their office's uppermost deck, the most expansive of the roof gardens.

Design Laboratory

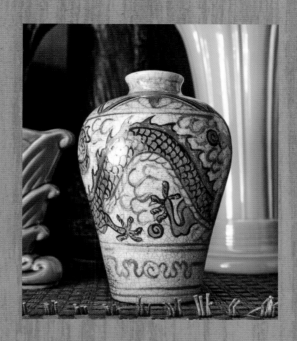

OUR HOUSE IS THE ARCHITECTURAL EQUIVALENT OF A PALIMPSEST.

Harwell Hamilton Harris (1903–1990), one of California's
highly regarded modernists, designed it in 1940 for Dean
McHenry, a political scientist and onetime dean of the
social sciences division at UCLA (while our parents were
undergraduates there), who later became the founding
chancellor of UC Santa Cruz. Sometime in the early 1960s,
a bad renovation for a new owner obscured much of its
original elegance and clarity. By the time we first saw the
place in the mid-1990s, it was in teardown condition, or
so said our families and friends. The house's history and

PRECEDING PAGES: With layers of variations, the exterior color palette in this outdoor living area takes its cues from elements of the interior. BELOW: In plan, it becomes clear that Harris oriented the house to emphasize the indoor/outdoor connection, encourage as much light into the interiors as possible, and frame a garden in the crook of each wing. With a rise in elevation, the pool area jogs off axis. We added the cabana for pragmatic reasons but also to provide a definite focal terminus to that vista. When we later built the pool house/guesthouse, we sited it to acknowledge the axial shift and reinforce the transition between the two distinct sections of the property.

remarkable bones captivated us, however. So did its many inherent garden opportunities. We knew that attempting to bring the property back to life would encompass huge challenges, yet the opportunity to reinvent it for our family while honoring Harris's intentions was irresistible. In the years since, like so many architects' homes, it has become a research and development lab for tinkering with ideas about residential structures, their interiors and gardens, and the indoor/outdoor relationship that is central to life in Southern California.

A onetime aspiring sculptor who decided to pursue architecture after visiting Frank Lloyd Wright's Hollyhock House, Harris had started his career in the offices of Richard Neutra. These legacies were instantly apparent in the way the different structural elements engaged the lot's inherent slope. The garage and original street-level entry to the house were (and still are) at street level. Stairs climbed (and still do) to the main living spaces. The pool and gardens occupied the rear of the property's higher elevation; there they remain, with our later additions of a pool cabana and pool house/guesthouse. As for the main house, its low-slung roof lines, floor-to-ceiling windows, glass expanses, board-formed concrete elements (including a massive retaining wall), and ease of access between indoors and the exterior spoke immediately of its intellectual heritage: what we coined "a Case Study House body with a Frank Lloyd Wright roof."

Harris had laid out the house in a cruciform plan, which he oriented on the compass points. His original structure created four courtyards—four potential gardens—each with a different aspect. This meant that we could plan and plant each garden with a distinctive character that suited its particular location. Harris had also made nods to the Asian influences that were on the rise in design circles when he was working on the house: he organized the interior spaces on a three-foot by three-foot tatami grid, which became apparent when we succeeded, thanks to Brian's aunt, in tracking down the original plans. (Brian's late uncle knew and worked with Dean McHenry at UC Santa Cruz.) The second

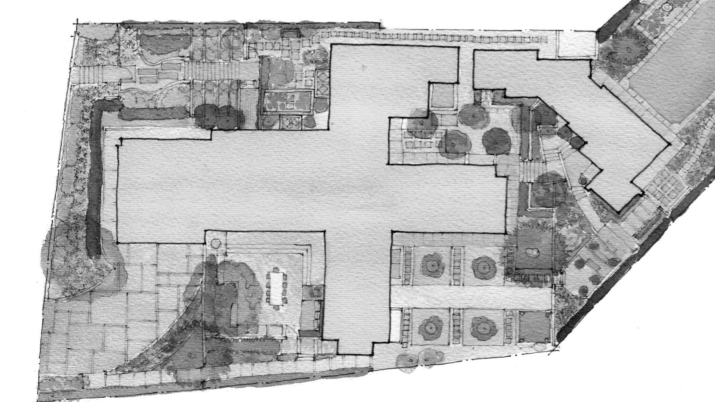

owners supplied the plans for the remodel. Nearly all of the original single-pane glass doors and windows were still in place, along with the original hardware. Traces of what may have been an early Japanese garden, in the form of a bamboo spigot, was all that remained of the upper entry garden. These elements became the cornerstones and leitmotifs of the renovation.

Architectural renovation is a process akin to an archaeological reconstruction. Because this house was modern, it did not have a plethora of design details as clues. Those that it did have, however, were specific and strong. Each room included several crucial elements in the original plans that needed accurate restoration for the house to regain its integrity. The first layer of the project involved peeling away the accretions and replacing the pieces that were singular and key. We restored the symmetry of recesses that flanked the living room fireplace, for example, because the earlier renovation had removed one of the recesses completely. Without that pairing, the fireplace—and the room—felt off-balance, rather like a missing twin.

Here, and in all our houses, each room pairs with a corresponding outdoor entertaining space, private space, pool, fountain, pond, or wild space. Harris's cruciform plan made that interior/exterior relationship organic from the outset: as every garden has walls on a minimum of two sides, every garden space is innately an exterior room

ABOVE LEFT: The exterior entry stair ascends through a terraced garden carved out of a formerly unused space on the side of the house. Dry-stacked concrete terraces and vintage stone troughs adjacent to the concrete treads create spaces for additional plantings, including vegetables and herbs. **TOP RIGHT:** Punctuating the border is an *Agave desmettiana* (smooth agave), one of several agave varieties we used throughout. **ABOVE RIGHT:** From this drawing came the built reality.

with its own narrative that relates to the adjacent interior. Thus, the living room and kitchen share a patio with an outdoor fireplace that sits on axis with the living room hearth, while the garden off the other side of the kitchen was our daughter's play space when she was young and is now planted with wild grasses divided by a bocce court that doubles as a path to the pool garden. One side of our master bedroom opens to a courtyard that connects to Brian's studio. The other unfolds into the reinvented Japanese garden with a lily pond.

In other areas of the house—the kitchen and the laundry room, for example—we elected to depart from Harris's original plan, although in our remodel we retained his detailing and aesthetic. The entry posed its own challenge, as it was key to the character of the house and to the process of reaching the living spaces. Harris's original plan called for a partially exterior (and very dark) passage up to the light—interesting and dramatic, but really not practical (plus it had deteriorated greatly). We decided to let in the light and line the steep entrance stair with our library, as there was no other obvious place to store our extensive collection of volumes. We also opted not to make any adjustments to the three-foot-wide hallway that serves as the house's spine. Though it presents some circulation issues, removing it would have destroyed the articulation of the original tatami grid.

With the pool, the compass orientation shifts because the property itself takes a directional swerve. We massaged the area into a cruciform plan of sorts as well, building the cabana stairs (which cascade to the pool) at one end over the nearly three-foot-high and very gnarly roots of an existing rubber tree. In recent years, we've added the pool house/guesthouse, which was inspired by many visits to the Mauna Kea Beach Hotel on the big island of Hawai'i. (Originally designed by Skidmore, Owings & Merrill, it is one of our favorite getaway spots in the world.) Here we've reinterpreted Harris's original leitmotifs and riffed on them, using windows quite similar to those in the main house, tweaked the ceiling to give the interiors a tropical sensibility, and decorated with furnishings, fabrics, and accents that remind us vividly of Hawaii.

We have made countless adjustments and reinventions, major and minor, to the house and all the gardens over the years. And we are deep into the planning stages for their various next iterations. A home—our home—constantly reminds us that we use it differently with each of life's phases. We feel it is imperative to respect its origins, especially when they have some historical significance. Yet it is just as important to know that when it's ready for its next act, we can change it.

At the upper landing of the entry stairs, planters with Little Ollies (dwarf olive trees) mark the access to a short bridge leading to the main house and frame a "secret" entrance to a hidden garden behind the bamboo fencing. *Wisteria sinensis* carpets one side of the fence; a pomegranate tree adds spots of color in front of the African fern pines on the property's border.

ABOVE AND OPPOSITE: Enclosing the original, six-foot-wide covered exterior stair was a major feature of our initial renovation. We appropriated one foot of depth along one side to create a library for a good portion of our extensive collection of architecture and design books; the facing wall serves as a gallery for artworks we've acquired over the years. The paintings on the bookshelves are by David Storey; a series of Brian's encaustic paintings hangs vertically at the landing. The window draws one upward to the landing; from there, one turns and ascends to the upper foyer.
OVERLEAF: The perspective from the upper entry foyer shifts to a view of the Japanese "secret" entry garden, the only outdoor room that retained any trace of its original intention at the time we purchased the house.

ABOVE: Along with many other elements of the living room's décor, a pair of carved Japanese lamps from the 1950s make direct reference to the traces of Asiana in the house's design DNA. **BELOW:** Vija Celmins's screenprint *Ocean with Cross #1* hangs over a grouping of vintage barware atop an expandable rolling bar cabinet. **RIGHT:** In the living room, the tint of the rug is foundational (and reminiscent of a swimming pool!). To furnish the house in a contextually appropriate manner, we opted to mix mid-century modern pieces such as the vintage Monteverdi-Young chairs (from a Palm Springs house) with classic contemporary upholstery forms and Asian furnishings and objects. The vintage Paul Frankl table echoes the strong horizontal lines of the house.

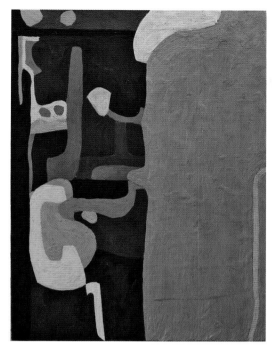

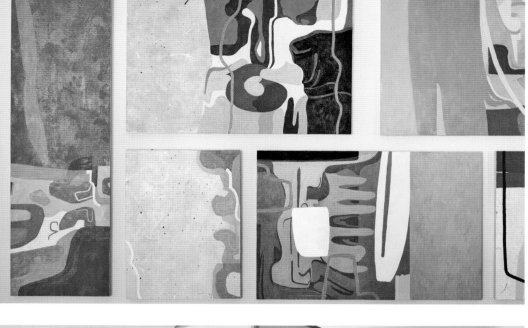

PRECEDING PAGES: The outdoor dining courtyard nests between the kitchen and the living room. In organic symmetry, its fireplace sits directly on axis with the living room hearth; this mirror imaging, along with the consistent color palette, helps tie the interior and exterior rooms together.
OPPOSITE: A quartet of capiz-shell globes hovers over our round dining table, squaring the circle, as it were. The opposite wall serves as a gallery for an ever-changing rotation of Brian's paintings.
ABOVE LEFT AND RIGHT: One recent series explores the qualities of encaustic on board.
BELOW AND RIGHT: Just around the corner from the dining area is the kitchen, which handily houses a full bar and butler's pantry.

ABOVE: Located in one of the rear quadrants of the house, the studio of our daughter, Ava, is large enough to include a space for studying and a seating area where she and her friends can hang out. The rug brings in the ultramarine from the living room. **BELOW LEFT:** For a feature wall, the overscale Lear Gaukur bird print helps to connect the interior with the world just beyond the wall of glass doors and windows. **BELOW CENTER:** Throw pillows elaborate on the palette and pattern elements overhead. **BELOW RIGHT:** Monkey the cat rules the roost. **OPPOSITE:** In Ava's adjacent bedroom, the bed takes in the long view through the *Nassella tenuissima* (Mexican feather grass) of her garden.

LEFT: One of the real virtues of the Southern California climate is that it permits outdoor activity all year around. As an outdoor destination, if not quite an exterior room of its own, this daybed is a sanctuary space at the far edge of the grass garden, near the plaster wall that encloses the pool garden. **ABOVE:** Pathways and a bocce court cut through the plantings.

ABOVE: Pat Steir's *From the Boat*: *Constellation* hangs over our custom-designed leather bed; Brian's closet is behind the striped-silk curtains. **BELOW LEFT:** Vintage millinery doubles as art atop the built-in mirrored dresser in Raun's closet. **BELOW CENTER:** The master bath benefits from the flow of natural light. **BELOW RIGHT:** Vintage books, such as these by Cecil Beaton, often serve as inspiration for our work. **OPPOSITE:** Mirrored cabinetry and a leopard carpet (which Monkey thinks is his mother) bring more than a touch of glamour to Raun's closet. **OVERLEAF LEFT:** Opening off the bedroom, Raun's sitting room/ office overlooks the Japanese garden; vintage Japanese obis and a 1930s batik from Brian's maternal grandmother hang from the bookshelves. **TOP RIGHT:** On the brushed-brass tabletop, the room's essential palette of ebony and ivory finds expression in a variety of scales and materials. **CENTER RIGHT:** In an ode to mid-century modern, the miniature Eames La Chaise chair feels right at home amid the stacks of Hermès boxes. **BOTTOM RIGHT:** An Asian lidded box holds exercise paraphernalia.

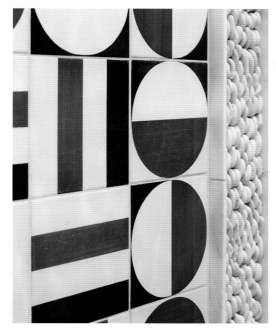

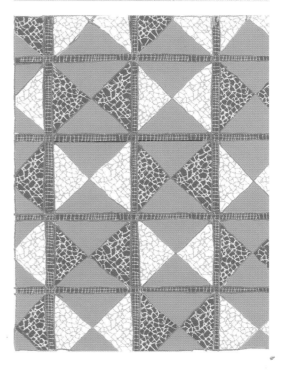

OPPOSITE: Two of our passions are Gio Ponti and Asiana; both converge in the spa fountain. An anniversary gift to Brian, the vintage 1960s tiles are Gio Ponti designs made originally for the Parco dei Principi Hotel in Sorrento. They certainly feed into the color story that threads its way through the property, and we spent months arranging and rearranging the pieces to find the pattern that we felt best suited the location. In the Asiana department, marble lotus flowers and Indian carved-stone carpet weights that serve as finials add additional form and texture to the cast-concrete coping. **THIS PAGE:** Texture and pattern are obviously related, sometimes closely, sometimes not. Throughout, we've used both to create understated yet interesting expanses on vertical and horizontal planes. **CLOCKWISE FROM TOP RIGHT:** The pool house floor is a terrazzo-and-limestone mosaic; a detail and a rendering of the pool house foyer's terrazzo-and-limestone floor; stained-concrete pavers inset into pebbles that are set on edge within a stone border in the master bedroom and studio courtyard; the on-edge pebble border flanking the spa's tiles reappears on the landings leading to the pool house.

THIS PAGE AND OPPOSITE: Brian's studio is a well-lighted haven for all kinds of creative expression. Here he works through the abstractions of form and composition that he explores as a painter and the representational illustrations that he uses to help communicate an architectural vision.

CLOCKWISE FROM TOP LEFT: A bed of succulents such as *Aeonium haworthii* (pinwheel) seems so simple, even monochromatic, but a closer look reveals abundant complexities of color and texture; an early rendering of the terraces that ascend to the pool house entrance; a rendering of a low fountain visible from Ava's room and from the pool house stair; the "real thing," carved from Indian marble and set in a bed of gravel surrounded by *Aeonium* and *Echeveria*, with magenta *Phalaenopsis* blossoms afloat; *Phalaenopsis* also blooms in the cabana; *Aloe arborescens* (torch aloe) adds incandescent sparks of color. **OPPOSITE:** The entrance to the pool house is a riff on the entrance to the main house, with a discreet door under a projecting eave. Monkey keeps watch.

OPPOSITE: In the pool cabana, the turquoise and tangerine palette and the Asiana elements of the design find their apotheosis. **ABOVE:** Our design for the pool house incorporates key references to Harris's original design for the residence, such as the clerestory windows and projecting eaves; in elements of its interior décor and the way it opens directly onto the pool, it also nods to one of our favorite works of modern architecture and vacation spots, the Mauna Kea Beach Hotel. **BELOW LEFT:** The handmade traditional Hawaiian quilt on the bed comes from the big Island of Hawai'i. An antique camphor chest, brought from the Philippines by Raun's paternal grandmother, sits at the foot of the bed. **BELOW CENTER:** The double-height foyer serves as a library; the shelving also conceals a drop-front desk and a tiki bar. **BELOW RIGHT:** In a neutral palette with its bamboo wallcovering and dark accents, the bathroom provides a serene getaway from the sun. **OVERLEAF:** On axis with the cabana, the sliding doors of the pool house retract completely into the wall, creating the ultimate indoor/outdoor space when they are open. *Brugmansia* blossoms overhang the garden beds and perfume the pool area.

Every designer describes each project and the design process in singular terms. For us the entire project, house and garden together, tends to be a philosophical and physical puzzle, or series of puzzles. Of necessity, the thinking that goes into each carefully crafted solution factors in a multivariable calculus: programmatic requirements, creation of a design narrative and/or parti, physical parameters, budget, local codes and regulations, and the different natures of static structure and living landscape. The design process, alternatively, resembles a chess game—or, for the botanically minded, a "decision tree." Similes aside, choice (and the soundness of that choice) is the fulcrum on which the process turns and develops. That's why intensive analysis is imperative.

Which design move do you make when you don't know or can't be sure what new series of challenges it will trigger? Such are the conditions of the puzzle's first layer. Resolving them means considering each apparent option, trying to foresee all the possible consequents, and imagining their various permutations. Working through them one by one, and then in in an integrated way, yields insight into the exponential potentialities to come. Some seem foregone. Some surprise. Some pose interesting conceptual risks. Others drop out of the gambit almost immediately. Following each through to its logical conclusion helps identify those essential design ideas—the "design DNA" or narrative—on which the project will pivot and develop. The process also illuminates whether, and how, a choice connects to the myriad others. And that in turn indicates what sort of editing or selective pruning of ideas may bear the best possible design fruit.

The challenge of finding opportunities where none may appear to exist, or where taking advantage of the obvious prospects involves an exceptional degree of difficulty, raises the complexity of the thinking. Intensive analysis usually reveals possibilities that may lie deep beneath the surface and indicates a way to thread successfully through the labyrinthine web of regulations, codes, aspirations, and desires that forms the calculus of each architectural undertaking. Gamely re-navigating each series of hurdles, attempting different resolutions, and, if necessary, reconceiving not just the possible solutions but the essential definition of the puzzle itself helps ensure that in the end the project has real meaning and a distinct design strategy. This is true whether the undertaking is a from-the- ground-up house and garden or a historic renovation/ adaptive reuse. It is also important to remember that sometimes answering a question has nothing to do with actually solving a problem, because they are not always the same thing. This happens all the time, and very often during construction. In such instances, the first move is not to move. The second is to figure out the best possible resolution(s). The point is never to feel trapped while remembering that every move has consequences that may cause ripples later in the game—and that's part of the process too.

Every project, no matter how well planned, always takes its unexpected, unpredictable turns. This might involve a complete change of mind about a decision made early in the process that is fundamental to the project's conception and layout. Or it could be an agency that rewrites its zoning regulations and so rescinds an approval six months after it's been given. As with everything in architecture, the possibilities for such glitches are practically infinite. Yet they're often when and why the very best design happens.

Suppose, for example, that the lot has been cleared and the building of house and garden can begin. Yet in the time between planning and permits, a large tree that affected the siting of the house has died. That change to the landscape offers a late-stage opportunity to twist the house more toward the view, which would substantially improve the majority of the overall design. But that same move would shift one room, a home office, in front of another tree, a potential disaster in the making. During the planning and pragmatic decision making, certain pieces of the wish list for the original puzzle—a rooftop spa to take advantage of the view; a structural element that felt like a tower; a home office set somewhat apart from the rest of the house—had of functional necessity given way to others. This late-in-the-game swerve now put them right back on the table. Splitting off the office into its own tower of sorts not only solved the problem but also restored parts of the dream for the property.

For us, the life of design lies in the strange twisting and turning that comes with trying to puzzle out each piece of a project so that it fits as perfectly and harmoniously as possible into a whole that exceeds all expectations. And we love it.

PUZZLES

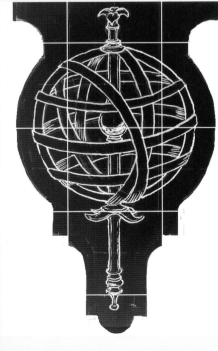

In the Frame

WE ARE VERY FORTUNATE IN THAT MANY OF OUR LONGTIME clients love to build. Some, like this couple, are deeply interested in exploring different styles of architecture and garden design from one residence to the next. For them, context is always a decisive factor in determining the development of each design. So are the contents they envision for their interiors. As passionate, informed art collectors who have amassed substantial holdings ranging across cultures, mediums, and eras, they edit their collections to suit the locations of their homes. For this house in Palm Springs, the two wanted to showcase their significant

PRECEDING PAGES: The plant palette of this desert garden includes Mexican fan palms, *Phoenix canariensis* (Canary Island palms), 'Orange King' bougainvillea, and *Aloe ferox* (bitter aloe). TOP: With its strong axial perspective and pool pavilion and spa framed by gardens, the plan of this modern desert residence takes its cues from the California courtyard version of the French Pavilion–style house. ABOVE AND OPPOSITE: An exterior entry foyer establishes the grid and frame motifs explored in the design; it also helps to modulate the desert light and provide a transition between the walkway up to the house and the front door.

collection of modern works by twentieth- and twenty-first-century California artists, as well as decorative pieces from a broad range of periods and cultures. They feel very strongly that the interiors of each house should be designed to frame and display their collections while simultaneously capitalizing on the views of the landscape's captivating features. They also love to make the most of the indoor/outdoor lifestyle that is the great gift of Southern California's climate. And they entertain frequently. All these intentions inform this Modern-meets-French-Pavilion-style desert getaway and gardens.

The property sits on a lot in Las Palmas, a historic section of Palm Springs near downtown that is full of the old palm trees that give it its name. It is also graced with remarkable views of the San Jacinto Mountains. The front of the lot, however, happened to face the mountains, which meant that if we situated the house's main garden with its central courtyard and pool (the "backyard") in its conventional position, it would not get the benefit of the most captivating vistas. The challenge of the orientation presented us with a key question: how best to organize the overall design back to front? By creating a long, palm-lined drive leading all the way to the rear of the lot (an idea inspired by Gordon Kaufmann, one of Los Angeles's great, early twentieth-century architects), we were able to establish a proper sense of procession to the entry and site the house in such a way as to open its heart to the peaks. In the newly established deep space behind the long, fenced drive, we introduced a strong axial plan to organize the outdoor living spaces—an entire secret garden of sorts—with a poolside pavilion, bocce court, and plantings, all arrayed around a central pool that reflects those glorious distant peaks on its surface.

Creamy, white, and full of light, the interior of the house features both very clean lines and an earthy feel, with decoration by John Cottrell. The public areas—kitchen, living room, and dining room, delineated, when necessary, by custom latticed pocket doors—flow in an open plan that extends via pale stone floors and pairs of massive, bronze-framed French doors to the exterior spaces, which include two trellised, partially covered terraces and an outdoor kitchen complete with pizza oven. The high-ceilinged living room gains additional daylight from a little interior courtyard next to it, but the room never gets uncomfortably bright. The art infuses the otherwise

understated interiors with color. In the gardens, the palette is as tightly focused as a painting: a flash of orangey red, typical of the desert flora, hints of lavenders, cream in all its nuances, and a full spectrum of grays and greens.

The couple had told us from the outset that they planned to display much of their collection of modern and contemporary paintings by California artists here, so we made sure to create interior walls and openings that are almost gallery-like in their ability to become both frame and backdrop for the art and the view. We also designed appropriate venues for specific pieces that we knew in advance were coming—a beautiful Helen Lundeberg, for example, and some spectacular works by John McLaughlin. Sufficient built-in storage and display space have been integrated into the interiors to accommodate extensive holdings of catalogues and scholarly materials.

The property also includes an unusual clump of twelve old palm trees, grown together at the base, which we have incorporated into the overall axial composition as a surprising yet necessary syncopation. Those palm trees, and a similar mass in the interior courtyard, provide a sense of place. Their age, plus that of an existing stone pine in one corner of the garden, makes the entire place feel very settled. A tall hedge around the entire property constitutes the largest frame and sets up the focus for additional layers and graduated perspectives into the grand borrowed view over the top of the neighboring palm trees and up into the mountains.

OPPOSITE: In contrast to the structure's strong orthogonal geometries, irregular quartzite paving carpets the transition from exterior to interior. ABOVE: With its lowered light levels, the entry foyer feels cool and calming, which allows the drama of the art and furniture to take over. The Los Angeles–based designer John Cottrell collaborated on the interiors. RIGHT: The upward view from the exterior entry frames the old palms that gave the neighborhood, Las Palmas, its name. FAR RIGHT: A vase of white peonies and magnolias picks up on the textural drama of the coquillage console and James Hayward's *Abstract #46*.

OPPOSITE: A high wall covered in *Ficus nitida* (Indian laurel fig) frames the perimeter of the property and serves as a privacy screen. Along the driveway, an understated gate set discreetly into the hedge offers an exterior entrance to the garden, which is a well-kept secret from the street. ABOVE: To make the most of the spectacular view of the San Jacinto peaks, we placed the house at the very rear of the lot and re-choreographed the entry to the front door via a long side drive (an idea inspired by the architect Gordon Kaufmann) lined with *Muhlenbergia capillaris* (pink muhlygrass). RIGHT: Like all designed spaces, gardens should have focal points; in this area, a sundial serves that purpose, drawing the eye to the spiky *Aloe ferox* that radiates around it. OVERLEAF: The primary axis engages the living room with a vista that encompasses the spa (set amid clumps of fragrant 'Lockwood de Forest' rosemary) and pool, then moves upward to the peaks and the high, broad sky beyond.

THESE PAGES: A strong, secondary cross axis extends from the side gate through the garden to the pool cabana, where a Moroccan light fixture introduces a touch of the exotic. OVERLEAF: Looking back toward the house from the far end of the pool, the symmetry of the structure becomes apparent. An allée of *Washingtonia robusta* (Mexican fan palm) reinforces the linearity of the property's plan; cascades of 'Orange King' bougainvillea add flaming color to the neutral palette.

ABOVE: The public spaces of the interior and exterior connect in a particularly fluid manner via a series of bronze-framed French doors and the patterned quartzite paving, which extends the reach of the living room out to the contiguous furnished terrace. Pairs of intricately carved pocket doors introduce the option of a bit more privacy into the interior's open plan (and keep the dogs enclosed when necessary). **OPPOSITE TOP:** The structure of the terrace frames the living canvas of the view in four directions, including overhead. **OPPOSITE CENTER:** Brian's sketch conveys the power of the grid and the nested rectangle, this house's design DNA.

RIGHT: A faux-bois concrete chair introduces a rather rustic, gutsy grace note into the surroundings. **FAR RIGHT:** Antique meets ancient in this vignette, where the whimsical vessel plays against the elemental hewn tree stump.

OPPOSITE TOP: The kitchen and interior dining areas occupy one of the two wings that abut the living room. **OPPOSITE BOTTOM:** Unfolding beyond the kitchen is a covered exterior dining terrace with a wood-burning pizza oven and grill. Container plantings of aloes and kalanchoes bring the garden up close and into the living areas. **ABOVE:** An early rendering clearly establishes the axial organization and processional approach. **BELOW LEFT:** *Kalanchoe beharensis* (velvet elephant's ear) stands out against the plaster wall. **BELOW RIGHT:** Foreshadowing the interior's wood pocket doors, this opening offers a glimpse into the courtyard.

ABOVE: This clump of palm trees outside the living room is one of two that were on the property when our clients purchased it. Both proved instrumental in our decision-making process about the overall plan of the house and the organization of its interiors. **LEFT, TOP TO BOTTOM:** Varying the pattern, texture, materials, and scale of the paved-stone carpeting underfoot is a way of subtly suggesting connections and distinctions among different areas. **OPPOSITE:** Even an early vision for this courtyard outside the living room included a stair to a roof deck focused on the commanding view.

ABOVE: The end-of-hallway spot where Helen Lundeberg's *Interior with Painting* hangs was conceived for art display. The painting on the left is Kim MacConnel's *Cara Dos Mil*. **BELOW LEFT:** Mary Corse's *Untitled* draws the eye to the bookshelves. **BELOW CENTER:** Karl Benjamin's *Vertical Stripes 2* adds a punch of color to the guest bedroom armoire. **BELOW RIGHT:** John Coplans's *SF6* focuses attention on the indoor/outdoor connection.

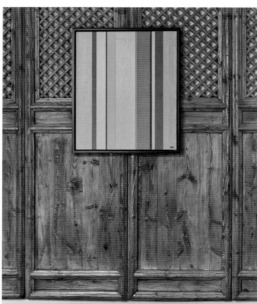

ABOVE: We designed the interior spaces in great part to show off this couple's substantial holdings of modern and contemporary California artists (including the John Sonsini oil above the mantel), but also factored in their wider interests as exuberantly eclectic collectors. The century-old Buddha hails from northern Thailand. **BELOW LEFT:** Collected finds layer the spaces. **BELOW CENTER:** Carved panels (three pairs serve as pocket doors) introduce an ornamental filigree into the interior that plays off the motif of the framed view. **BELOW RIGHT:** Marcia Hafif's *TGGT: LB 2 06* injects some cool hues into the mix.

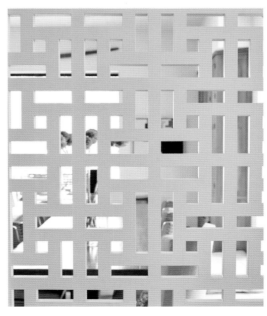

ABOVE: In the master bath, fire and water play central roles in the creation of luxury. The mirrored wall surrounding the stone fireplace brings the reflections of the outdoors inside. A nineteenth-century oil from the school of Paris hangs in dramatic contrast above the tub. **OPPOSITE TOP:** With the abundance of natural light, it made sense to create a protected niche for the master bed, which is open to the views but out of direct sunlight; Marcia Hafif's *Shade Paintings #1* introduces color over the bed; next to the bed is Scot Heywood's *Painting #89 Red*; by the window is Robert Dowd's *A 31*. **OPPOSITE BOTTOM:** With a floor-to-ceiling glass wall overlooking the private garden, the shower feels as if it's open to the exterior.

The landscape is a living canvas. And in any landscape, urban or rural, there are always places in its near, middle, and far distance that are more beautiful than others. Identifying these various focal points and panoramas is key to understanding the singular nature of that particular property—and why we design our projects from the outside in. A crucial part of the discovery process involves determining which highlights of the distant scenery—a mountain range, a palm grove, an ocean, a country club golf course—can be borrowed, framed, and incorporated into the sightlines of the house to enhance the overall visual composition of the property and extend its perceived reach out beyond its proper borders.

Conceiving a house by first envisioning its windows and what they face—the type of gardens, streetscape or landscape, and skyline; the axial vistas, allées, sunrises and sunsets, and the occasional surprises—means designing the house and the specifics of its gardens simultaneously to frame, create, and capitalize on the finest possible views morning, noon, and night. This entails thinking about plant palettes from the outset. To determine which plant varieties to use in a given location, one must know the properties and strengths of its soil. With experience, one can sift a handful of earth through the fingers and realize almost immediately what kinds of plants will work and thrive beautifully in precisely that spot. And so it becomes possible to imagine what the near, intermediate, and far views will be from specific windows.

Of course, gardens can be ephemeral too. But they often leave traces of their past. On a historic property, the ground itself can sometimes still give a précis of the story. On occasion we can discover, or at least conjecture, the long-gone plantings by seeing what has survived and reseeded itself. Then the question becomes whether that past is sufficiently important to replant for the future. Or whether in reinventing the garden, it might be preferable to underscore how things grow and change. The degree to which that makes sense is different for every project.

Gardens take twenty years or so to reach full maturity, so we conceive and plan for plantings with different life cycles to evolve into the structure of the garden through successive stages. There is a first version, the four-year plan. Then comes the middle iteration, which reaches fruition at about eight years. Finally, the garden grows into its long-awaited form for longevity. This phasing in of plant life over time is a major component of how we compose the specifics and details of the views. We design in the potential for a similar layering of nuance inside the house because it, too, evolves as it takes on the patina of the lives lived within it.

Scale plays a major role in determining the framing and content of each view, as plantings that enchant in one way when seen close up almost always change character when seen from afar. A swath of succulents, for example, may appear as a watercourse from a distance but like a tapestry from nearby. Sometimes container plantings, which also factor into issues of scale, prove to be the only viable option for a particular portion of the garden. Potting fruit trees and deploying troughs filled with succulents, for example, are one way to establish focal points and fold more layers of life into the larger landscape. Because they provide their own soil, they have the added advantage of creating opportunities for plantings where none might otherwise exist, such as in front of a wall surrounded by hardscape or in a restricted space next to a house on a narrow lot, all while simultaneously readjusting the view. Further, containers can keep the root systems of large flora in check, thereby preventing any disruption they could cause from negating the beauty that their presence adds. And because container plantings are also comparatively easy to move and replant at will, they offer built-in flexibility for a quick or seasonal change of scenery when the desire or need arises.

Even when we work in places with inclement weather or environments with a short summer and long winter, we still focus the design of a house and its rooms on the views framed therein. Once we know what we want to see at various points in the expanse toward the horizon, we can decide how best to organize and orient the gardens to reinforce the geometry of the property; how to site the house most advantageously; and how to place the outdoor living spaces to create as seamless a transition as possible. The goal, in the end, is always to delight the eye as near—and as far—as it can see.

VIEWS

Historical Convergences

WHEN MOST PEOPLE COME TO US WITH A PROJECT, THEY USUALLY have an informed sense of the periods and styles of architecture and design that they favor. Only once has someone come to us with absolutely specific (and utterly arcane, for those not in the profession) precedents in mind. This is that house. It results from the clients' twin fascinations with the late eighteenth-/early nineteenth-century neoclassicist Sir John Soane, the great Regency architect, and the seminal 1977 book *A Pattern Language*, by the widely influential architectural theorist Christopher Alexander, a longtime professor at UC Berkeley. We're still not precisely clear

PRECEDING PAGES: Reinterpreted through a contemporary lens, Georgian-style details endow the interiors of this house with timelessness and gravitas. OPPOSITE: For a house inspired by the clients' unexpected fascination with Sir John Soane and Christopher Alexander, a sense of neoclassical order and the rhythmic power of pattern merge in the design of the façade. TOP: An early sketch of the front façade makes clear how the design evolved through the development process. ABOVE: The motif established by the arched overdoor on the exterior finds expression in the vaulted ceiling of an interior hallway.

ABOVE: The pattern language of the interior begins with the essentials of straight and curved lines, of squares, triangles, and circles, and develops into a range of related geometries. BELOW: Diamonds, circles, and squares repeat in panel detailing, window muntins, marble flooring, and custom ironwork of the stair rail. OPPOSITE: In a nod to the architect Roland Coate, one of California's masters who brilliantly understood light and proportion, the foyer welcomes natural light from many different heights and angles.

OPPOSITE AND ABOVE: With detailing derived from the Georgian architect John Nash, the wood-paneled library features an understated flourish of animating ornament. A vintage Suzani covers the library table. The décor throughout the house is by the late Joe Nye.

ABOVE: On every plane of the living room, understated detail builds upon understated pattern. The effect reaches an apotheosis of sorts on the ceiling plane, where Georgian-inspired beading and reed work activate the surface and draw the eye upward. OPPOSITE: Ebonized moldings lend definition to the components of the dining room, creating a sense of embrace. The fireplace surround continues the Soane theme.

OPPOSITE: To create a sense of timelessness, the master bathroom incorporates all the modern luxuries with fittings and fixtures that hark back to the past. **ABOVE AND RIGHT:** Derived from an exemplar in Soane's Lincoln's Inn Fields house, the pendentive dome features beading and corner details. **FAR RIGHT:** Custom brass hardware in the master suite continues the beading.

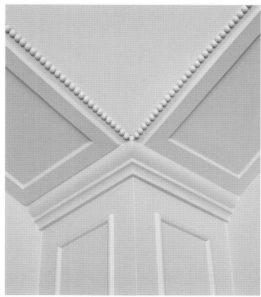

about how and why they became dazzled by these two legendary figures and their work. But that they were presented us with a completely unique intellectual challenge: to examine the two sophisticated aesthetic languages and determine where they overlapped.

We knew that once we found the consonances, we would have starting points for a grammar that we could interpret and build on for the residence. Soane and Alexander share some interesting ideas about the compression and expansion of space (for each, there are literal rules). Both also deal with the idea of developing design through thematic, telling detail. So while exact parity between their individual philosophies and aesthetics doesn't exist—how could it?—there are subjects on which they do at least correspond. These provided a basic framework for the project's intellectual superstructure.

The other primary force in the development of this design happened to be its context. The lot sits on a corner in the heart of Pasadena, a block from the Cal Tech campus and very near the Huntington Botanical Gardens in San Marino, a beautiful old residential community. The entire area is rich in architectural history. So we turned to nearby precedents for inspiration and were able to bring much of the local architectural history to bear.

We based certain aspects of the house—one of the late Joe Nye's final decorating projects—on the work of Johnson, Kaufmann, Coate, a Pasadena firm in the 1910s and '20s that was tremendously influential in the early development of an indig-

OPPOSITE AND ABOVE: In a play of different scales and materials, the pattern language in the family room follows a neoclassical proportional system, which is expressed in the paneled casework, in the cabinet over the fireplace mantel, in the window muntins and mullions, and in the ceiling coffers.

ABOVE LEFT: The English-inspired kitchen has views of the garden at both ends. A wood-topped work table abuts the stone-topped island. **TOP RIGHT:** A study for an alfresco dining terrace and herb garden. **ABOVE RIGHT:** The central courtyard brings sunlight into most of the house and also creates a fair-weather outdoor living room around its fireplace.

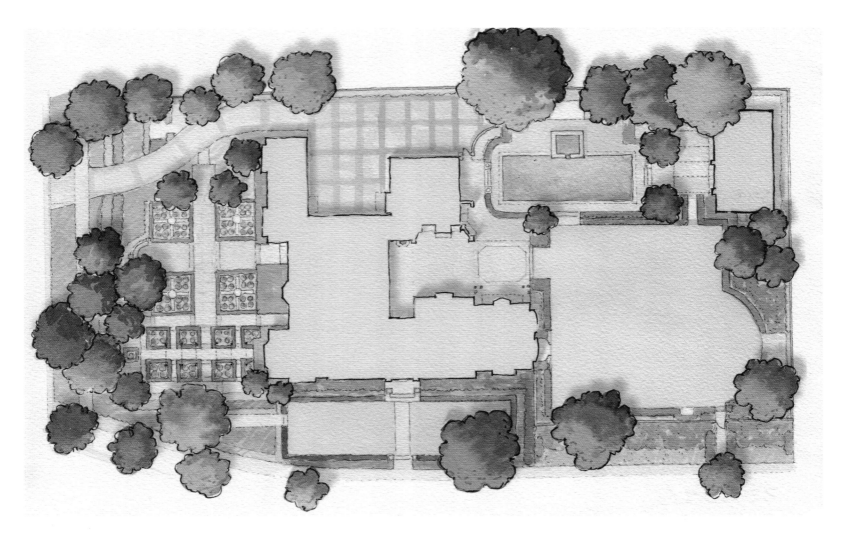

This house sits neatly on its site, maximizing both interior and exterior living space, as well as gardens and views. We took numerous cues from the century or more of rich architectural history that characterizes this area of Pasadena.

enous architectural style for Southern California. That firm was a training ground for Paul R. Williams, H. Roy Kelley, and many other seminal twentieth-century California regionalists. When the partnership broke up, Johnson, Kaufmann, and Coate each went on to individual greatness. But for insight into the composition of this house, the way it presents itself to the street and occupies the lot, we took some important lessons from the work of Roland Coate, a greatly underappreciated talent who was deeply involved in the development of the Monterey Colonial style in the 1930s. A master of proportion, he was incredibly inventive in resolving the issue of entry and its relationship to the stair hall, of directing light through the interior, and of establishing a sense of enfilade. Early in our careers, we had remodeled and designed an addition for one of his notable projects, the Vinmont estate in Los Feliz. We also looked to Bertram Goodhue's plan for Cal Tech. And we quoted some plantings from the remarkable Florence Yoch's work on that campus.

In the plan of the house and all the detailing, Soane, Alexander, and the Southern California masters converge. From panel trims to molding to balustrades, ceiling treatments, floors, fireplace mantels, hedges, spa, and pool, essential geometries reoccur in various scales and dimensionalities, always with delicacy, restraint, and understatement. In the master suite, our design debt to Soane is finally made overt in a beading detail that subtly animates the ceiling and the hardware. That quiet reference to the Regency especially delighted the master of the house. To us it feels both timeless and of this time.

RIGHT: An early iteration of the pool and pool pavilion placed the structure at the terminus of the axis. **BELOW LEFT:** A fountain set into a courtyard adds the element of sound. **BELOW RIGHT:** A development drawing of the pool garden.

OVERLEAF: View of the pool garden from the master bedroom terrace. Palms, magnificent California live oaks, and distant, sometimes snow-covered mountains complete an archetypal Pasadena composition.

OPPOSITE: Capped with three Georgian urns, a demilune bench provides scale for the garden, as seen from the kitchen window. **ABOVE:** In the rose garden, a long, arched trellis creates an illusion of greater depth. **RIGHT:** A built-in garden bench adds human scale and a sense of habitability to the large rear garden.

Charles Moore, an architectural history savant if ever there was one, was at home across the global chronology of built culture. Georgian, Italian Renaissance, Sultanate Delhi, you name it, he could discuss any given style in terms of period, context, and philosophical influences—and all in deep, meaningful detail. He often said that it was possible to take defining elements from any/every era, culture, and style, find the links, put them together, and make something better. This kind of historically informed invention has always seemed a good philosophical approach to architecture and design that applies equally to all types of projects.

Simply put, we are history buffs. Eclecticism and inclusiveness, plus respect for and sensitivity to context, form the core of our particular approach to design and construction. A shared passion for precedent pushes us to try to understand at the most basic level how each form and every detail of architecture works in whatever period, culture, style, and individual intelligence has shaped the design. Only with that understanding does it then become possible to translate those forms and details into the present tense. This holds just as true for "modern" structures as it does for those inspired by or reclaimed from any one of the older traditions—from which, of course, "modern" (and everything else) descends.

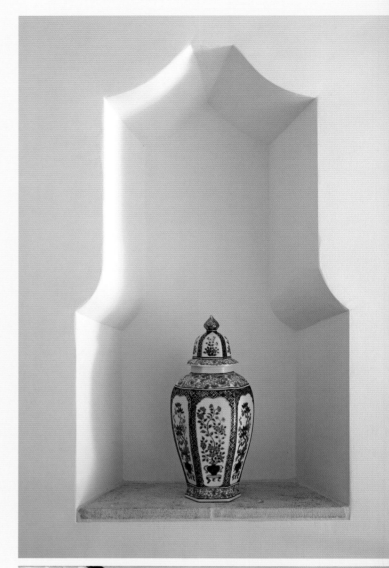

The story of American architecture may be comparatively short, but it incorporates a broad range of borrowed or inherited influences and transplanted traditions. In California, it is arguably more polyglot than in other regions because California architecture assimilates Asian idioms along with the hybridized English, French, American Colonial, and Spanish-inflected traditions that dominate the domestic landscape.

Interestingly, the high Mediterranean style and the English- and European-infused ultra-classicism of California's great, early twentieth-century estates actually comes into existence alongside an emergent California Modern tradition that reaches full bloom a generation later. Tracing back both branches of design and intellectual influences to their roots, it becomes quite evident that they hail from the same tree. That simultaneity characterizes the real California tradition. And it is inseparable from the modern garden, which knits together the interior and exterior.

When an opportunity to reinvent an existing structure presents itself, an architect dreams in a very specific way. The hope is always that the building and garden retain enough traces of telling original detail to inform and amplify any design choices for the present and the future. In Southern California, a sense of deeper time emerges when one reuses what stands to formulate a way forward. There is also, obviously, a moral imperative to keep the landfill from growing. What resonates most of all is the feeling of honoring other lives lived and making something out of their something, of recasting it in our own time. It is impossible to replicate that experience. For a ground-up property in a traditional mode, these same qualities and considerations come into play, though quite differently, as an informed vision, rather than a surviving archaeology, leads the way.

Accretive solutions for historic projects (or any existing project, for that matter) usually go one of two ways, aesthetically speaking: they can be either conjunctive or disjunctive. The choice tends to be a philosophical one that factors in client desires, design review parameters, and zoning and other regulations. Including allusions to the depths and dimension of the project's origins is, more often than not, our preferred choice. But either way, in the archaeology of place the challenge remains to develop a fully formed concept of what needs to be. When there is a piece of history, we are going to keep what we can and build on it, instead of wiping it clean.

Because precedent and inclusiveness are the essence of who and what we are as architects, a well-stocked and continually updated library is a necessity. But it is one thing to read about a place or a structure and research it extensively through photographs and ongoing scholarship. It is quite another thing to read about it, understand its history, and then experience the reality of that place. Only through travel is it possible to discover the emotional and physical truth behind the precedent, to comprehend the essence of how a certain structural arrangement of materials, volumes, colors, forms, and so on looks, feels, fits into its place, and is engineered down to the smallest detail—and how our bodies respond to it. That understanding enhances our ability to modulate the qualities and sensory pleasures of the spaces we create. For like everything else in architecture, what matters is the reality of being there.

HISTORY

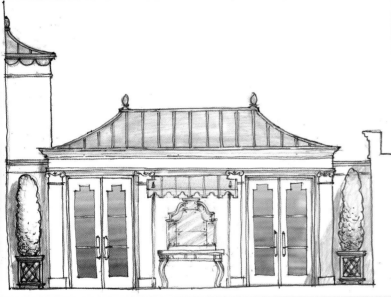

True West

OVER THE YEARS WE HAVE WORKED WITH OUR VARIOUS FAMILY members on a number of their residential projects. This one happens to fall into the Thorp camp: brother, sister-in-law, niece, and nephew. Although they're based in New York, when they began searching for a place to build a second home they opted against the Hamptons. He's an avid fly fisherman. She's a passionate hiker and outdoorswoman. They wanted their two young children to know and appreciate the great outdoors. And so they explored westward. As soon as they set eyes on Jackson Hole, Wyoming, they fell in love with its remarkable landscape.

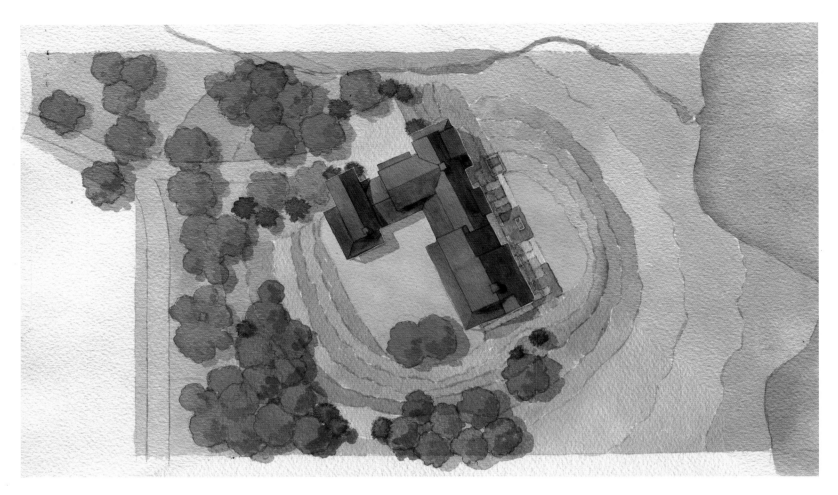

PRECEDING PAGES: Western references woven into a more broadly global mix give this lofty living room its distinct personality. ABOVE: From the property lines to the interior core of the house, this design takes maximum advantage of the views. On the approach to the house, a winding lane lined with aspen, cottonwood, pine, and silverberry offers various perspectives on the landscape. OPPOSITE TOP: The house sits lightly on the land. OPPOSITE BOTTOM: With deep eaves and covered porches, the house incorporates iconic elements of farmhouse and ranch vernaculars in a recognizably modern reinterpretation.

By the time they found a suitable property, they had conceived of the idea of a modern farmhouse. They envisioned it as a two-season retreat and also as a place where the extended family would gather. Their land offered spectacular views of the Tetons, as well of a pond and a network of creeks running into the Snake River. But their community, like many developing communities, had established very specific design review guidelines in addition to the existing municipal codes and regulations. Caveats included materials (a menu of stones and woods), rooflines (pitched and with deep overhangs), the number of wood-burning fireplaces (one per building), and native plantings. And because the entire area was under a dark-sky ordinance, there were also strict standards for exterior lighting. All of these guidelines necessarily informed our thinking about the house and its gardens.

Researching the iconic American ranch and farmhouse vernaculars helped us clarify our thoughts on what a hybrid modern version of those forms might be, as well as what native plantings would be suitable for the surrounding gardens and landscape. Over time, an airy, light-filled, two-story retreat began to take shape. The ground floor housed luxe, high-ceilinged public spaces—living room, dining room, kitchen—with occasional rustic elements; a suite specially designed for visiting grandparents; an additional guest room; and a gym with a view of the Tetons. On the second floor, the master suite, children's bedrooms, a home office, and a den were arrayed in single file off a long hallway. A stand-alone guesthouse adjoined the main house via a large, covered breezeway. And an 8,000-bottle wine cellar, connected to the kitchen, had its own private, two-story domain.

Plan-wise, laying out the first-floor rooms in an open enfilade made sense both for the way the family intended to use these rooms and for connecting the interiors to certain focal points in the view to make the most of the panoramic sweep. One side of the house was left quite open to the exterior, unfolding to a furnished terrace and outdoor fireplace, as well as to an outdoor dining area with a barbecue. The

THIS PAGE: The massive stone hearth grounds the soaring volume of the living room, while the wood-paneled ceiling with exposed wood beams adds warmth and detail. Other visible structural elements contribute to the modern ranch vocabulary, as do some of the more rusticated finishes. **OPPOSITE:** For a casual meal or a game of cards or chess, a glass-topped vintage table next to the window wall feels appropriate in scale and reflects the view.

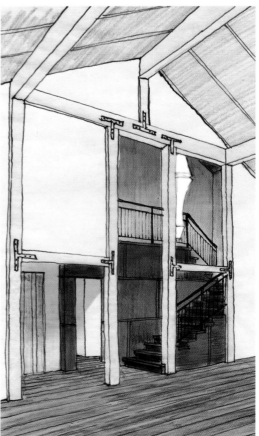

other side, framed by the guesthouse and the main house, was enclosed a bit more with a berm, native cottonwoods, and pines to create a protected lawn/play space for the children.

Within the enfilade, a spatial choreography of compression and expansion moves people from room to room and to and from the outdoors. A capacious, ranch-style front porch leads to the front entrance, a substantial barn door that opens to a small foyer. The first view is of the central hearth in the double-height living room and the surrounding landscape through the tall windows. The adjacent dining room flows into the open kitchen. All of these rooms are oriented so the light streams in from more than one direction.

We also designed the interiors of this house. Throughout, natural materials are at play alongside iron and steel. As the family's taste tends toward the more pared down, we kept things understated but added warmth and texture with paneled ceilings, wide-plank wood floors, and light fixtures that had some relevance both to their modern aesthetic and to the broader context of the West. Specific furnishings and accent pieces clearly refer to the locale without tilting the décor toward the slavishly Western. A few items, like a collection of framed vintage bandannas, and the occasional antlers and faux animal heads, introduce notes of tradition and humor.

In the living room, the furnishings, decorative accents, and architectural details explore the contrast between the occasional rusticated surface, high-tech materials, and the classic modern, mid-century modern, and contemporary pieces that they particularly love. Framed on two sides by large expanses of glass doors and windows, this room's generous volume meets the big sky with its own plays on horizon and scale. The stone hearth and paneled ceiling with its wood beams add warmth and texture, while the great balls of light that are the capiz-shell pendants help to bring the perception of vastness back into human scale. With two seating areas around the fireplace, plus a table and chairs near the window, the space works equally well for intimate and large groups in a variety of relaxed pursuits.

Because the dining room is open to the kitchen, all the kitchen surfaces are visible, so they all matter. From a distance, the kitchen's white and stainless-steel finishes make it appear to dematerialize. But the wide-plank walnut floor and bleached-walnut panels overhead help to fix it in space and also riff on the farmhouse/ranch house theme.

The wine cellar distills the design elements of the house to their essentials: polished stainless-steel racks, sophisticated lighting, and curated collection. Slate floors and Nakashima-style chairs continue the modern/organic themes, as do the recycled

PRECEDING PAGES: The house is see-through, but in contrast to its more circumspect front façade, the rear is wide open to the view and unfolds into the landscape via furnished outdoor living spaces. **OPPOSITE:** With a long, live-edge, claro walnut-and-bronze dining table, leather-topped wood bench, and lacquer-and-walnut sideboard, this gathering space incorporates the family's favorite earthy modern designs. **TOP:** In spirit, the exterior fireplace corresponds to the interior hearth and has a similarly focusing effect. **ABOVE:** With these views, who wouldn't want to while away the hours on the treadmill?

ABOVE: Through a perspective sketch of the kitchen, the relationship between the ceiling and cabinetry grids becomes immediately apparent. **BELOW:** Under a trio of Brian's encaustic paintings, a folding tray table in the kitchen offers a handy place for additional storage or a pretty still life. **RIGHT:** With so much space overhead and views of the landscape all around, the wood-paneled ceiling and the constellation of pendant fixtures create a sense of intimacy and connectedness to the earth.

PRECEDING PAGES: A screened porch with indoor/outdoor furnishings provides a protected spot for drinks. A vintage French bottle-drying rack hangs on the far wall. **LEFT:** A covered breezeway connects the guesthouse (on the left) to the garage and offers covered passage to the house in inclement weather. **ABOVE:** Petite and made of resin, the pair of antlers in the guesthouse entry doubles as a coat rack; it's just one of many small, functional decorative elements that speak to the context.

OPPOSITE: A favorite of our sister-in-law, this Gee's Bend quilt adds a happy graphic punch to the guesthouse living room. **ABOVE:** The Los Ojos coral wool Pendleton blanket that covers the bed brings a gutsy gravitas of bold color and elemental pattern to this guesthouse space, which includes many references to iconic Western designs. To accommodate relatives and friends who visit with their children, a sleeping loft hovers overhead.

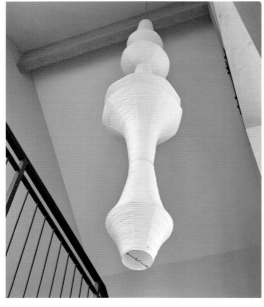

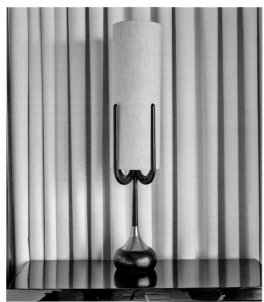

TOP ROW, LEFT TO RIGHT: A Noguchi light sculpture from Akari provides scale in the main hall stair; oversized capiz-shell fixtures hover like planets over the great room; a steel basket sconce with a hand-finished patina brings a touch of rustic glamour. **CENTER ROW, LEFT TO RIGHT:** In the master bedroom, a vintage Modaline lamp atop a lacquered nightstand introduces another riff on the antler theme; a ceiling pendant adds a rigorous filigree; in the master bath, faceted lanterns play off the tracery motif. **BOTTOM ROW, LEFT TO RIGHT:** In the first-floor powder room, the mix of materials includes wood, hide, and leather; cherry wall sconces insert both modern and organic notes into the second-floor den. **OPPOSITE:** Metal master Curtis Jere made the mirror in the master bedroom, where another Pendleton blanket introduces references to Native American motifs.

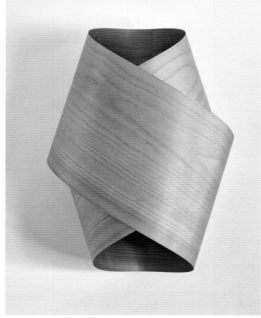

LEFT: Fine wool casement curtains (a riff on bed hangings) enclose or expose one of the master bedroom's breathtaking vistas, to which the four posts of the Christian Liaigre bed serve as a framing device. The hide rug introduces a now-meets-then, here-meets-there resonance of sophistication to the mix of periods, textures, and styles. **ABOVE:** Hans Wegner's Papa Bear chair brings the mid-century into the mix. **BELOW:** German lacquered chests with hand-inlaid brass scenes bring arboreal and fauna references indoors.

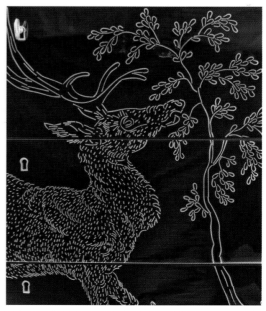

ABOVE: In the master bath, modern luxury prevails with a tub angled just so for surveying the snow-capped peaks.
OPPOSITE: On the second floor and down the hall from the master suite, a home office emphasizes the "modern" aspect of the "modern farmhouse" narrative with a telescope that looks across to the Tetons, a horn side table, and Le Corbusier's classic modern chaise in cowhide.

OPPOSITE: In our nephew's room, Pendleton blankets from Glacier National Park cover twin beds reminiscent of camp bunks. **ABOVE LEFT:** In our niece's bedroom (she did think pink), a capiz-shell fixture resembles a cottonwood blossom. **ABOVE RIGHT:** The children's rooms are joined via a Jack and Jill bath.

BELOW LEFT AND RIGHT: We couldn't resist the vintage bandannas, which introduce additional notes of pattern, color, and touches of Western wit and whimsy. **BELOW CENTER:** Small and cozy, the upstairs den occupies an expanded landing.

wine-barrel tops that compose the floor's hexagonal parquet.

A retreat of redoubtable peace and calm, the second-floor master bedroom is nuanced in its color palette and sophisticated in its furnishings, mixing elegant exemplars of contemporary simplicity with mid-century icons and modernist classics. When the wool casement curtains behind the bed are opened wide, the bedframe acts as a viewfinder to focus and direct the eye toward the remarkable landscape. On one side of the room, French doors open onto a balcony that looks out at the pond, mountains, and big sky beyond. The master bath is a retreat unto itself, with a minimalist stand-alone tub angled to take in the breathtaking view.

The great swaths of carefully calibrated natural grasses planted early on have begun to establish themselves in their intended layers. As they continue to flourish, they will create a melding into the landscape beyond the mown lawns and the berm next to the house, and past the reintroduced gooseberry, cottonwoods, and pines. This family residence was one of the earliest in the area. When we originally oriented and planned the house and gardens, we wanted to try to ensure that the windows would not look out solely on eventual neighboring houses. As the place has become more populated, the grasses and trees continue to grow into magnificent maturity, enfolding the house in a layer of privacy and tying it organically and seamlessly to the age-old landscape.

OPPOSITE: With its combination of sleek industrial and earthy organic elements, the two-story wine cellar distills the intellectual and aesthetic reasoning that underlie the design of the entire house. The slate-floored tasting area glows under a tea paper ceiling. **ABOVE:** The cellar accommodates 8,000 bottles in custom shelving units. **RIGHT:** In the second-floor bin storage area, the surface underfoot consists of recycled wine-barrel tops set in a hexagonal pattern. **FAR RIGHT:** Custom-lighted display racks line the stair. **OVERLEAF:** With great swaths of native and horticultural grasses and trees, including cottonwoods, aspens, and pines, planted in carefully calibrated layers, the property melds into the broader landscape.

Looking at the history of America—and especially the American West—through the lens of the landscape, the effects of evolution, cataclysms, and civilization are all writ large. Two environmental stresses in particular—fire and drought—have factored deeply in the past century and a half of drama in what is arguably our American Eden. Yet these same two elements of fire and water are essential to sustaining life and habitability. Embedded into a landscape, they provide a visceral beauty, besides. And so we parlay them, carefully and consciously, throughout our invented vistas, outdoor rooms, and gardens.

We know practically by heart so many stories of the pioneers—the wonders they witnessed, the hardships they survived—as they pushed a young nation westward across the majestic span between the Atlantic and the Pacific. Yet the experiences of explorers that predate our own time can take some serious digging in the archives to discover. It is easy to overlook that when the first Europeans wandered into (what is now) the Los Angeles Basin, for example, in August 1769, they documented a perfect place: the ground covered with roses, streams meandering, abundant trees, and green grass as far as the eye could see. In the 10,000 years prior to their arrival, this extraordinary climate sustained more people per acre in the Americas than anywhere other than the Mexico City Basin. Surely these people tended fires under the open skies, cooked over them, and gathered around them in the darkness for light, safety, and community. Contemporary fire elements—fire pits, outdoor fireplaces, outdoor kitchens and grills—provide similar comforts out of doors today, especially when positioned at a remove but in harmonious relation to indoor living and dining areas. Not only do they pragmatically introduce scale to their surroundings, they create practical focal points in the deeper landscape around which to orient exterior rooms where people may gather at any time, but particularly on chilly nights. In the broader spaces of the West under the endless sky, they bring the spirit of the campfire into the present.

In Mediterranean climates, even the slightest trickle of water welcomes, cools, and calms whether visible up close or seen and heard from a distance. The same holds true across the West, but perhaps particularly in Southern California, where the Mediterranean aesthetic has taken root on the shores of the Pacific over the last century and a half. Here, because of drought, design must find a way to enhance the effect of each and every drop of water. But no matter where we work, we scale our water elements to the gardens they enhance. We're cognizant that it takes only a little bit of moving water in a fountain, rill, or spa to achieve an outsized effect in a courtyard or elsewhere. It is not just the water alone. It is the reflection of light off the wet surface, the floating leaves dropping from overhead, or the aquatic plants that a fountain or pool may sustain. There are also the dragonflies that the water attracts, the way they skitter across the surface and enliven the atmosphere with their fluttering wings.

When a water element enters the landscape, like a fire element it recalibrates the scale and refocuses the experience of the space it occupies and all the areas around it. So how to accomplish even more while keeping the water usage in check? Disarticulating a property's various wet components—separating the spa from the pool, for example—doubles the purpose of the individual elements. In this way, a spa becomes a fountain too.

The goal is always to create an integrated vision of the landscape, so the color of the water plays an important role in the overall balance. The classic California pool—kidney shaped and otherwise—tends to be lined in white plaster so that the water reads as turquoise. Tinting the plaster may lead to a more harmonious composition among all the elements: pool, landscape, garden, and even the architecture of the house. For a traditional house with a French accent, for example, French gray plaster yields pool water close to a navy blue. For a Portuguese-inflected house with a classic blue-and-white interior, a light French gray creates a pool of cerulean blue. The use of sand-colored plaster in the pool can make people as if they're at the beach. The options are almost endless.

A number of the more expansive gardens that we have designed over the years include a variety of water features scattered through the landscape, everything from fountains to pools to spas to a half-acre pond. Yet the largest garden we have ever created—it spreads across a six-acre compound with five houses—contains not one single water feature among its many outdoor elements and destinations. Twenty years ago, early in the conceptualization phase of this property, a feng shui master ruled out the use of moving water anywhere on the site—not even a fountain. At the outset, the prohibition seemed to pose a quandary. But necessity truly is the mother of invention. And discovering alternate ways to evoke the same effect with swaths of plants and establish the garden's focal points by other means became its own source of fascination. The absence of water drove home so much more clearly what the presence of water, even in the smallest of quantities, can and does mean to everything around it.

FIRE and WATER

Creating the Dreamscape

AS PROJECT NARRATIVES GO, THIS ONE COULD HAPPILY READ as: "Ralph Lauren goes to Normandy" in order to meet "Sabrina comes to Los Angeles." To understand how our design actually twists, turns, and reinterprets these references, it helps to know the backstory.

When we began working with this family, they were living in New York, expecting their third child, and planning to transplant to their native California. Early on in our discussions, he made his love of both the French and English architectural and garden traditions clear, as did they both about their desire for a certain degree of glamour. That's

PRECEDING PAGES: Axial vistas are essential to the design of this house and its gardens. ABOVE: For clients who wanted a house that brings glamour to historic precedent, we channeled the residential traditions of Burgundy and England, as well as their reinterpretations via Hollywood. BELOW: The living areas push to the edge of the one-acre lot but incorporate gardens and a view borrowed from the adjacent golf course. OPPOSITE TOP: From low to high, graduated hedges of dwarf mock orange, Japanese boxwood, and true myrtle create a stately, living architectural surround for a fountain accented with an Indian carved-marble jali. OPPOSITE BOTTOM: Light streams into the foyer from various levels.

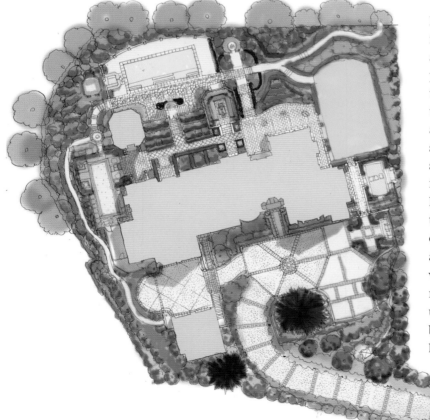

when we found ourselves not only turning to traditional features of Norman residential architecture and certain aspects of the houses of Edwin Lutyens as jumping-off points for the project, but also folding in the interpretation of those precedents in the great estates of the East Coast and their translation into comparably grand West Coast properties of the 1920s and '30s. (It's worth pointing out that this couple cares so deeply about history that they insisted on having scholarly documentation of the historical precedents so they could understand how we were planning to use them in a non-historical way.) And that's also when we introduced them to their decorator and art consultant, Thomas M. Beeton.

The most significant design issue involved the question of how to realize such an ambitious residential dream—one that included a substantial house along with a pool, outdoor living and dining areas, not to mention a pool house, a freestanding pavilion that is a chinoiserie gym, gardens, and so on—within the confines of a single acre. Compounding this challenge was the problematic lay of the land: not only was the buildable area nearly thirty-five feet lower than the point of entry at the street, but the driveway was disproportionately long for the size of the lot (a seeming difficulty that we exploited by creating an approach worthy of a far larger estate). Fortunately, the lot also contained two intrinsic benefits that helped mitigate the drawbacks. First, the slope was such that it allowed us to design a series of descending terraces for various destinations and features. Second, the lot bordered on a golf course that was particularly well landscaped with mature trees, including many pines and eucalyptus, among other species; this provided us with great opportunities to borrow distant views and blur boundaries in a way that made the entire property, but particularly the garden, feel as if it extended well beyond the lot lines.

To underscore the design intention of a house that feels completely cohesive yet functions in many different ways, the ground-floor interiors extend into the landscape through a progression of contiguous exterior rooms and destinations. Beyond the family room is a covered dining terrace with an outdoor fireplace. That terrace flows into an open-air dining area adjacent to the kitchen; a neighboring kitchen garden overlooks the pool. Just steps from the dining room, a roof garden atop the pool house takes in the entire panorama; with an exotic, Moroccan-inspired outdoor seating area arrayed around a fireplace, it reflects the spirit of a Continental adventurer bringing home remembrances of far-flung travels abroad. Upstairs, the interior/exterior paradigm continues. The entry's curved stair leads up to a landing with a view through the gardens and the pool area to the country club golf course and panorama beyond. The master bedroom has its own terrace, which overlooks the decrescendo of garden terraces below. The master bath peers into an exotic white garden with jali fountains and carved-marble panels. The interior architecture further reinforces the outward orientation by establishing focal point upon focal point, with axial views and enfilades that stretch to the gardens.

Both the interior and the exterior spaces have their own choreography of compression to expansion, of intimacy to generosity, of shade to light, of predictable to unexpected. Manipulating the ceilings is part of our technique for establishing a rhythm of spatial experience indoors. Outside, we institute a similar effect by layering the space with unexpected moments and defined destinations adjacent to well-established pathways.

We recently renovated and expanded the kitchen/family room wing, which allowed us to revisit decisions we had all made when we (and the couple's children) were

OPPOSITE: The wood-paneled drawing room takes cues from the English tradition. It also nods to an American precedent: a Stanford White–designed room bathed in modulated light from all four directions. Los Angeles–based decorator Thomas Beeton is responsible for the interior décor. **THIS PAGE:** From initial sketch to rendering to reality, the design for the paneled surfaces emerges in broad strokes and fine details.

younger. Because they use this area daily, in the years since the house was built they have developed a fine-tuned understanding of the evolving nuances of utility, function, and style that best serve them and their maturing children. This taught us all so much. In essence, we transformed what had originally been a traditional and rather formal area into a more modern and streamlined, yet still quite glamorous, interior where much of their everyday family life takes place. In addition to switching out cabinetry and finishes, modifying the way the island works, and reconfiguring various other work spaces, we added an ample breakfast/informal dining area to accommodate the larger groups that family meals now encompass. This is an aspect of the ongoing design narrative that never fails to thrill. As the garden grows, so grows the family. As they grow and their lives change, the property needs to change as well. It is our privilege to have the opportunity and the experience to make that happen.

OPPOSITE: A silver-leafed tea paper ceiling and soffit surround faced in antiqued mirror suffuse the family room with the glow of reflected light and an understated glamour that complements the patina of the hand-finished wood paneling. **TOP AND ABOVE:** A recent renovation to reflect the family's evolution re-envisioned the kitchen in white marble, tints of silver, antiqued ribbed mirror, and leather barstools— materials, details, and finishes that also resonate with the adjacent family room, which centers its focus on the hearth and the gardens beyond.

OPPOSITE: The paneled wainscot provides a grounding for the decorative flourishes in the formal dining room. Hand-painted panels by Dana Westring provide a scenic backdrop for Hovsep Pushman's *Life's Treasures, No. 515*, ca. 1940. ABOVE: In the powder room, where fantasy prevails, moldings and trim give Dana Westring's artistic flourishes a strict, comprehensible rhythm.

OPPOSITE TOP: To create convenient indoor/outdoor adjacencies, the kitchen and family room open to the dining loggia. Wisteria provides a verdant, cooling canopy of shimmer and shade overhead. **OPPOSITE BOTTOM:** The bocce court of decomposed granite and its adjacent seating area establish a destination at the far reaches of the property, where eucalyptus trees form a scrim that layers the vista into the adjacent golf course. **ABOVE:** A pair of concrete benches beside the bocce court creates a conversational nook. Bruno Romeda's *Untitled Circle #250* takes aim at the farther view.

ABOVE: Each ground-floor interior room unfolds via French doors to a corresponding exterior living space that provides a transition into the gardens and beyond. OPPOSITE: In the living room, a shaped plaster fireplace surround frames an antique French limestone mantel, introducing additional layers of detail to the French-inspired mustard-colored walls. OVERLEAF: A secret, walled garden is framed by tall, lush growths of sweet bay and loquat and animated by the plash of water from the inset fountain.

ABOVE AND OPPOSITE TOP: For pleasing spots of color and complementary scale, Moroccan jars bracket the Indian marble panels inlaid with floral motifs that have been inset in the walls of the secret garden. Within its coping of French Jura stone (used throughout the property) and boxwood border, the lily pond offers an essay in design symmetry. **OPPOSITE BOTTOM, LEFT TO RIGHT:** An early sketch for one of the panels; a detail of one of the garden's hand-carved Indian marble panels; a concept drawing for the floor in the master bathroom.

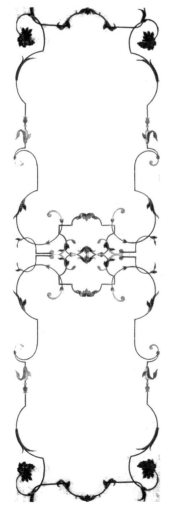

LEFT AND ABOVE: In the master bedroom, a tray ceiling accentuates the volume under the roof's slope. Pairs of French doors open to the furnished terrace. An antique rose marble mantelpiece frames the fireplace, which occupies a spot directly on axis with the room's entry.

RIGHT: Glamorous and practical, mirrored closet doors conceal storage and provide a reflective entry to her sitting area. **FAR RIGHT:** Like a carpet, the custom pattern that animates the mosaic floor of the master bath is contained within strict tile borders that shimmer with mother-of-pearl inlays. **OPPOSITE:** Set into a window bay created for the purpose, the tub offers captivating views in all directions and a view into a garden designed specifically for glimpsing from on high. **OVERLEAF:** The house is built on a rise. Atop the pool pavilion, an outdoor seating area inspired by the idea of "Moroccan Modern" overlooks the terraced layers of the planted landscape and into the borrowed view of the adjacent golf course.

ABOVE: The design of the pool area reinforces the symmetry that is an essential aspect of this property's design DNA.

OPPOSITE, TOP RIGHT: An early sketch of the pool area gives a sense of the property's slope and also the underlying balance between indoor and outdoor areas, garden and hardscape, structure and open space, and passages and focal points. **CENTER RIGHT:** An early iteration of the planning for the pool pavilion's roof garden offers insight into the puzzle pieces of this property's different levels. **BOTTOM RIGHT:** An early concept sketch of the pool area explores options for the custom-designed awning that shades the poolside dining area.

ABOVE LEFT AND LEFT: Throughout this property, the ironwork gates and fencing elements reinterpret traditional French and English scrollwork and arabesques in a contemporary aesthetic. **ABOVE:** Gardens descend down the slope to the property line in terraced layers, each with differentiated stopping points and destinations for sitting, viewing, and relaxing. Manicured hedges of coast rosemary line the pathways and express the garden's underlying architecture.

ABOVE: An early idea for one of the property's custom gates. **BELOW:** An early sketch for the finial-topped gates at the entry to the driveway set the precedent for the pattern language throughout the property. **OVERLEAF:** To make the property feel larger, we borrowed the view from the neighboring golf course, layered the garden plantings, and created paths between the various beds to offer more ways to traverse the landscape. The successive tiers also help to hide the golf course fence in front of the eucalyptus trees.

ENGAGING *the* LAND

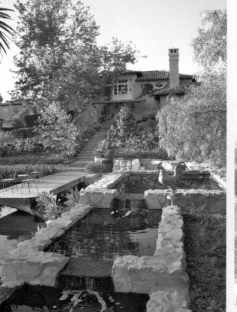

In placing a house—or any kind of building—on a piece of land, the first question is always how to site it. Two basic possibilities exist. One involves positioning the structure so that it dominates everything that it surveys. The other entails orienting the building so that it engages with its surroundings to the property line and beyond. In our opinion, the latter offers numerous design advantages, foremost among them the chance to create a cohesive vision of place that embraces both house and gardens. Practically speaking, engaging the land allows the structure of the building to extend into the garden much more fluidly. This enhances the quality of the views from inside the house into the garden and from the garden into the house.

Each from-the-ground-up project obviously begins with an inquiry into precisely the kind of house desired. How should it feel? Is there a preference in terms of period precedents and cultural references? Are there stylistic elements of the architecture that should factor into the garden discussion as well? What would be the optimal scheme, size- and style-wise, given the zoning, building codes, and existing regulations? These questions help inform the imagining of the site as a whole, as a private world. We want to ensure that within the lot lines there are no awkward or leftover areas around the house. Taking a page (and an ideal about planning and composition) from the precedents of the eighteenth century, we work to capitalize on what many might consider merely residual, odd, or unusable slivers of space. In such a world, the interior of the house relates to gardens that are completely appropriate to the exterior of the house.

When existing space is tight, a landscape can knit the close and distant views together by engaging the land, scaling and manipulating close-up vistas, and borrowing distant panoramas to compensate for the lack of expansiveness. This kind of scenic orchestration ensures that a variety of visual experiences unfold in as many directions as possible, from as many vantage points as possible, all the way to (and from) the horizon line. For this, the gardens must take an appropriate form, relating organically to the siting, proportions, and style of the house that created the spaces for them and also blurring the boundary between the scenes in the far distance and those up close. All of this evolves from the particular relationship between the structure(s) and its land.

Layering the landscape so that the design events unfold into and through it—and claim every last inch of it—helps develop the all-important sense of close, mid-range, and distant views. This also informs the perception of the overall scale of the individual spaces that these views represent. If a property encompasses a slope, for example, terracing the man-made experiences (including gardens and water features, whether rills, pools, or fountains) along the natural gradient not only helps to ensure that the constructed environment is completely in tune with the existing landscape but also makes the entirety of the site feel more expansive. This strategy for lying lightly on the land also provides destinations that draw people into and through the landscape and pathways to reach them. It further pulls any views beyond the property lines into the property's perceived scope. If no slope exists, then establishing even a slight change of grade for the garden can enrich the property's character, providing a feeling of enclosure, or separateness, or destination.

Just like the interior, the exterior feels habitable when it includes places to sit, places to visit, and destinations, like a cabana, gazebo, or pool house, for lingering a good length of time. The Mediterranean tradition offers rich precedents—Gallic, Spanish, Italian, and the like—for layering the landscape around the house in ways that American designers have been reinterpreting since the late nineteenth/early twentieth centuries. The California Modern legacy, much more recent, offers fine examples as well, particularly with regard to the seamless transition between indoors and out. And the English, notably, have long been masters at shaping the scenic landscape. Over the centuries, they have developed their culture of houses and gardens, inserting follies, gazebos, allées, fountains, walls and hedges, gardens, mazes, and so on into a property to engender a variety of experiences, spaces, and views that range from the refined and cultivated to the organic and wild. Our Californian interpretation of that tradition might look something like this: A long drive leads to a house where the front door opens on a formal, circular foyer, the fulcrum from which public rooms extend in an enfilade in both directions and a graceful sweep of stair ascends to the second floor. Each ground-floor living space unfolds to a corresponding exterior space that flows organically into the living landscape that radiates around the house; each second-floor room opens to an outdoor space as well. Pathways into the property's farther reaches suggest various destinations and wind through plantings that terminate in exterior events: a succulent garden, a rose garden, a fountain, a pool and pool house, a pergola-covered exterior dining terrace, an outdoor kitchen, a fireplace, a daybed or a hammock, and so on. Strategically placed seating at intervals suggests that the passages from one point in space to another are also places with purpose in and of themselves. In design, the power of suggestion is all.

From the Sea to the Stars

DESIGNING A HOUSE FOR ONE'S PARENTS IS A TRUE LABOR OF love, as we well know. One of the first projects in our partnership was the rebuilding of the Tichenors' beach house just north of Santa Barbara. About a dozen years later, we designed this two-story quinta topped by a small tower for the Thorps. Set on a tight but spectacularly situated lot high atop a hill, it faces endless unobstructed views in all directions, including a breathtaking vista to the Pacific.

The first inkling of the idea emerged on a cruise we all took together to Spain and Portugal not long after we were

married. Dr. and Mrs. Thorp were quite taken with the Portuguese variations on the classic Mediterranean courtyard house, and in particular the quintas we visited in Estoril, as well as with that country's interpretation of the blue-and-white ceramics that Mrs. Thorp had long collected. Some years later, with their life moving into a new phase, the idea of a house based on that trip reemerged.

Because we knew their wants and needs so well, and their many collections so intimately, we were able to think through every last detail of this place in a way that ensured that their existence once they moved in would be exactly as they wished. That said, compressing their lives into a house forecast to be slightly more than half the size of the one they were leaving behind presented a formidable challenge. So did figuring out the intricate puzzle of how to place and display their various collections, prized works of art, and family heirlooms, as well as their copious library. There was also the matter of integrating Dr. Thorp's ideal observatory. Working with them (and us) on the furnishings, fabrics, and details of the décor was Thomas Beeton, the Los Angeles-based interior designer.

ABOVE: A reinterpretation of a Portuguese quinta, this house incorporates elements from that most Mediterranean of vernaculars into the ease and comforts that characterize the California lifestyle.
BELOW: Through careful massing, the structure fits an expansive footprint into the lot's tight confines.
OVERLEAF: Our intimate familiarity with the Thorps' collections allowed us to tailor the design in places for the display of favorite pieces, such as the antique carved Chinese stone panel in the foyer. We based the designs for the custom ironwork balustrades and gates on precedents from Portugal and Spain. Los Angeles decorator Thomas Beeton collaborated on the interior décor.

Conceiving of a two-story structure that would function seamlessly and effortlessly as a one-story house, we organized all the essential rooms, from kitchen to master suite, on the ground floor. The inclusion of both stairs and an elevator made for an easy ascent to the second floor, which encompassed Dr. Thorp's office (and observatory) and two guestrooms. Because they were very private people, and because the footprint of the house was so compact, it was more than ordinarily important to delineate a hierarchy of public and private zones.

To fit the house and its gardens as graciously as possible within the constraints of the lot size and shape meant practicing some sleight of hand, design-wise. Though the exterior space was limited, the views were anything but, so we oriented the rooms to

incorporate their vistas in ways that made the scenery feel integral to the structure. By the same token, fully resolving the edges of the property and all the side yards helped to suggest that not only was the outdoors easily accessible, but that it was also expansively layered. Placing the pool in the front garden provided a further means for evoking a quality of spaciousness.

The entry sequence maximized the experience of procession: through the gate, past the entry tower (actually a small bathhouse for the pool), into the loggia, beyond a contained, four-square garden in the front of the house that frames the view to the pool, and through another gate on axis with the grotto. (We modeled the main entry gate after some gorgeous Portuguese grillwork seen on that trip so many years ago.) Near the pool with its shell grotto fountain, a spa that feels like a fountain is built into the front perimeter wall.

Everywhere the eye turns it alights on details, from ceiling medallions to moldings, from wall niches to floors, all derived and reinterpreted from Portuguese and Mediterranean precedents. Many of the walls incorporate fields of decorative azulejos, which enliven the understated surfaces with pattern and ornament and reinforce an overall blue-and-white palette sparked by the transplanted collection of ceramics. Brian spent a year painting the more than two dozen decorative tile panels that activate the wall surfaces throughout the property. The imagery resonates with themes inspired by the Thorps' lives and travels, and by the ideas that fed into the design of the house itself. He also did all the coquillage in the grotto. Together, we created the armature for the antique armillary sphere in the kitchen/cutting garden.

As we said, this house was a labor of love.

OPPOSITE: With a central starburst medallion and articulated beams, the dining room's octagonal ceiling recasts the room's foundational geometry and introduces Moorish references that are in keeping with the Mediterranean design motifs.
ABOVE: The indoor/outdoor connection is especially pronounced in the public areas of the house, such as this casual dining area, an extension of the adjacent loggia and a nod to European orangeries.

ABOVE: Like its cousin in the dining room, the antiqued iron and rock crystal chandelier in the living room picks up on the play of rustic and refined that is intrinsic to the architecture of the house. **RIGHT:** The floor plan is choreographed to capture both ocean and garden views, as the orientation of the living room windows makes clear. In plaster and limestone, the mantelpiece that anchors the room offers a modern gloss on a classic Portuguese form. **BELOW:** Mrs. Thorp's extensive collection of blue-and-white porcelains sets the interior's dominant palette.

ABOVE: Light, bright, and fresh, the kitchen is a favorite spot, with blue-and-white azulejos that infuse pattern and color into the mix of natural materials. **OPPOSITE:** Just off the kitchen, the octagonal breakfast room picks up on the geometric motif established by the ceiling of the formal dining room.

ABOVE: Framed by limestone pavers and surrounded by *Westringia fruticosa*, the greensward that unfurls off the living room loggia directs the eye toward the endless view. **BELOW AND OPPOSITE:** With its large hearth and outdoor seating, the living room loggia provides a protected outdoor area for conversation, a cocktail, or time with a good book. Octagonal columns reiterate one of the interior's animating geometries. **OVERLEAF:** Like the ground floor's other areas, the family room is oriented to frame the view and offer easy access to the garden. The grid of the coffered ceiling, another Portuguese reference, provides an organizing device for the placement of the room's overhead lighting.

OPPOSITE: Mrs. Thorp's office houses a portion of her extensive collection of art books and literature, among her great passions. It opens to the entry parterre, with a view of the pool and shell grotto fountain beyond. The antique camphor chest was brought from the Philippines by Dr. Thorp's mother. **ABOVE:** Limned in shades of blue and white, the master bedroom features several distinct areas demarcated by the varying ceiling lines. A soft arch, for example, frames a mini library with built-in shelves (out of view) and a chaise facing the ocean. **LEFT:** In the ground-floor powder room, vintage crystal sconces flank a Portuguese-inspired vintage mirror that reflects the hall library. **RIGHT:** Hand-painted tiles and a paneled vanity imbue the guest-suite bath with pattern and texture.

Dr. Thorp's second-floor office encompasses an extensive science and mathematics library and his private observatory, designed by Tom Melsheimer. Its retractable roof exposes a phenomenally powerful telescope that he uses to observe and photograph the constellations, planets, and other astronomical objects and events. A spiral stair ascends to the tower with its 360-degree views.

LEFT: In plan, the house wraps around itself, rather like a nautilus shell, to create interior courtyards, gardens, and the pool area, where Brian applied the coquillage and painted the tiles on the poolside grotto. Hedges of Japanese boxwood inset with 'Mystery' gardenias, plus plantings of star jasmine and 'Setsugekka' camellias, line the walkway to the pool. **ABOVE:** In such tight quarters, a lap pool made perfect sense. Surrounded by Aleppo and Canary Island pines, it feels completely secluded. Brian also painted the Portuguese-style blue tiles that are set into the pool's rear wall and border a built-in spa.

LEFT: The master bedroom spa, with its custom swagged iron handrail and more of Brian's hand-painted tile panels, takes advantage of a narrow side yard and reflects the endless sky over the sweep of the Pacific Ocean. **ABOVE:** Planted throughout the garden, torch aloe blooms spectacularly in the late winter. **BELOW LEFT:** An early rendering of the master bedroom spa explores the seamless integration of landscape and hardscape. **BELOW RIGHT:** Dense and spiky, *Agave attenuata* (fox tail agave) provides an element of verticality at ground level.

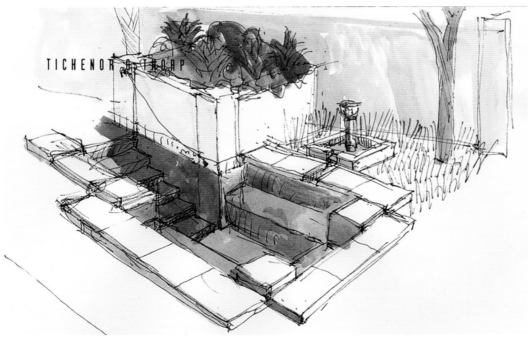

Inspired by the azulejos that adorn so many Portuguese quintas, Brian decided to paint a series of decorative blue-and-white tiles and panels that we could install throughout the property in spots where the images would have particular significance. Motifs include specific garden flora (*Aloe ferox*

in urns atop pedestals, Italian cypress by the entry); Dr. Thorp's fascination with astronomy (the armillary sphere and constellations); and references to the aspects of the cruise (schools of fish, Roman ruins) that originally inspired this house.

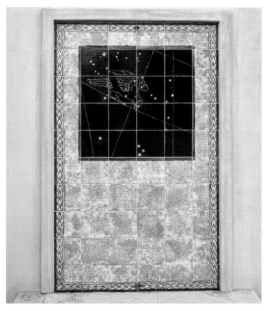

ABOVE: Both of us worked on the coquillage of the armillary stand in the kitchen and cutting garden behind Dr. Thorp's workshop, where another octagonal reference makes an appearance. Antique concrete finials top a dry-stacked concrete wall that borders beds for vegetables and herbs. This garden also contains pink David Austin roses, fig trees, and several types of citrus, including orange, Bearrs lime, and Eureka lemon. **OPPOSITE:** This path between plantings, one of a network of paths that circumnavigates the house, ends in a cul-de-sac enhanced by an antique Indian marble birdbath. **OVERLEAF:** The view from the cul-de-sac captures the hardy garden on the bluff, with Aleppo pine, trailing rosemary, torch aloe in full, flame-throwing glory, agave, and *Aeonium arboreum* 'Zwartkop'.

Each project encompasses a unique syntax of pattern that informs every aspect of its design, indoors and out, structure, hardscape, and living landscape. From foundational elements to decorative flourishes, the particulars of that pattern language emerge from the project's narrative as well as from deep research into, and analysis of, any precedents that help to inform it. Developing the pattern's individual components—its grammar and vocabulary—involves a constant negotiation between plan and elevation, horizontal and vertical, and two-dimensional representation and three-dimensional form because the same arrangement of linear components appears to be one thing when flat and quite another when it has height and depth.

Pattern operates on many levels in addition to the purely decorative. Because the design of any pattern in two dimensions is a kind of plan in miniature, it becomes another piece in the three-dimensional puzzle of the project's overall composition of compression and expansion, of the rhythm of the individual spaces and their volumetric relationship. Pattern also provides punctuation, depth, texture, and focus to any given expanse. Depending on its nature, it can tease and delight the eye in many different ways. But it should always serve to reinforce the design intent. In this way, the fenestration on a façade, for example, reads both as a distinctive organizing principle of transparency in structural solidity and as a signifier of that project's source of inspiration. Perhaps no other design component offers quite as many clues to a project's intrinsic character as a window. The quantity, scale, type, shape, and framing details of the apertures make reference to any and all precedents for a contemporary building as well as any broader historical sources of inspiration in terms of time, place, and design style. As windows are also defining for the interior's quality of space and light, they offer an ideal of the merger of pattern with functional purpose.

The form and meaning of a project's patterning develops from the outside in. In plan, many of our houses come into existence around a center or core. Some have spiral plans that resemble shells; others emphasize an axial organization; still others embrace a courtyard. This allows for each to have its own type of garden and a distinctive view that we hope to embrace, protect, or create in one or more aspects. From the panorama of the vast night sky and rugged mountain peaks, for example, we might intuit a grid with stars and angles that repeats throughout a property in various iterations, some more subtle than others, at different scales and in different materials, plant life included. A recurring waveform and depictions of marine life that ebb and flow throughout a house and garden in greater or lesser degrees of obviousness may hail from a distant vista of the ocean as well as from a travelogue that sparked the story for that particular house. A delicate beading expressed again and again, at appropriate scales, in moldings, trims, and hardware, as well as in a handful of forms out in the landscape may hark back to a historical precedent that inspired the entire project.

Some repetitive geometrics—grids, zigzags, stripes, and concentric circles, to name a few—feel elemental to the development of visual language across cultures and eras. Some patterns could just as easily project as Japanese, Spanish, or Greek as Native American, Moroccan, or Hawaiian when tweaked slightly in color palette, symmetry/asymmetry, and materials, and when lifted out of their native geographic and chronological contexts. Textural analogues to such polyglot patterns also exist. An arrangement of pebbles or river stones within a frame of a garden border might conceivably suggest Andalusia for those steeped in the arcana of garden design. But in all probability Japan would come to mind more immediately because of Japan's long and well-known tradition of raked Zen gardens. When that pebbled landscape features dark and light river stones set on their sides in a formal Euclidean arrangement, however, it could just as easily hail from the Mediterranean. How we understand it depends on the surrounding details and materials.

Intrinsic as it is to the design of both interior and exterior, pattern offers yet another means for translating the narrative of the project into its built expression through the choice and layering of the details. What the actual pattern consists of and how much and how obvious it becomes throughout a given property depends on the taste of the owners and on the nature and style of the house and garden. Some types of design schemes inherently call for an infusion of pattern, especially as surface ornament, particularly to provide a layering motif in a variety of scales. Others do not. Just about anything is possible depending on the precedent, for modernist and traditional legacies offer equally rich potential for reinterpretation. In the appropriate form, material, and expression, pattern reinforces the overall design even as it adds clarity and depth.

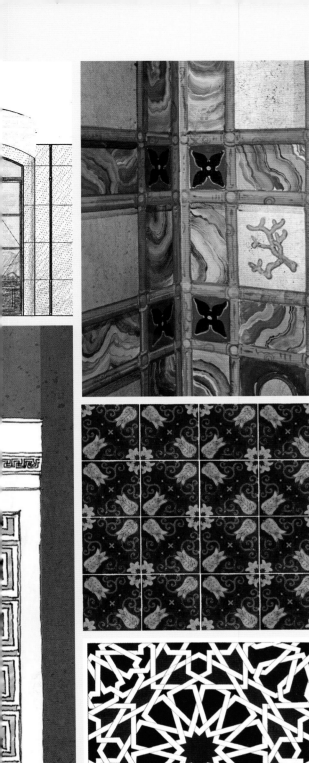

PATTERN

Continental Divide

THIS LONGTIME CLIENT, A HOLLYWOOD WRITER/DIRECTOR/ AUTHOR, began hunting for a New York City pied-à-terre when his college-age twins headed east. His good friend, a fellow director, introduced him to this three-bedroom apartment in the far West Village. The place appealed to him for many reasons, among them the promise of a river view. What clinched his decision was the apartment's proximity to Hudson River Park with its brilliantly landscaped bike path (he's an enthusiastic cyclist).

A somewhat strange amalgam of a studio and two one-bedroom apartments, the overall space suffered from

PRECEDING PAGES: Our bi-coastal client has an eye for mid-century design, a passion for light, and a love of the outdoors. In the redesign of his West Village residence, we wanted to satisfy all three. A vintage orange pottery urn transplanted from his California residence greatly influenced the interior's color palette. **ABOVE:** By tearing down some existing walls and opening up the public living spaces, we were able to carve out a reading niche with a quasi-library sufficient to house Vladimir Kagan's aerodynamic chaise adjacent to the living room area. Along with the orange urn and the vintage kilim underfoot, Brian's painting helped to set the color scheme for these rooms.

a truly problematic floor plan, among its many significant challenges. To say the place needed revamping would be an understatement. But in one sense, the architectural revisions were actually the least of it. Because of his profession, he gave exceptional significance to the design narrative: each scheme that we developed—and there were many—required its own tale. That said, the major plot points of this renovation were fixed from the outset. He needed an area where he could write. He wanted a reading nook. He liked modern. And earthy elements. And the expression of natural materials. And places for his children to stay on their frequent visits.

Before we could address the details of the décor, we had to resolve two glaring spatial challenges. The first was the location of the powder room, which was originally just adjacent to the entry, where it backed rather gracelessly into the living room. We relocated it to the end of the main hall, where, with an additional door, it now also

serves the guest bedroom. To hide the leftover plumbing, we designed a macassar entry piece (meant to serve as both bar and book storage) that created a new entry and framed a reading niche in the living room. We also cleaned up the apartment's core—specifically the circulation space—to further reinforce the separation of public and private areas.

The second spatial hurdle was the kitchen, a shoebox of a workspace that was visible from the entrance. After sifting through numerous possibilities for an alternative kitchen scheme, it became clear that the best solution was literally to think outside the box by removing the walls around it and exposing the functional aspects of the space to the rest of the apartment. That decision in turn begged the question of whether a separate dining room was necessary. Once he said "no," we proceeded to establish a quasi-loft-like open plan with a white, minimalist kitchen that unfolds

ABOVE: We used rugs to bring order to the open floor plan and establish the boundaries of each individual area; setting the stage and providing a dose of quiet pattern for the living area is a modern interpretation of a classic Moroccan berber. The pair of lounge chairs and the Vladimir Kagan–designed coffee table echo the low-slung lines of the chaise longue. Above the sofa hangs a piece by the Russian conceptual artists Komar and Melamid.

ABOVE: The original kitchen was a typical New York apartment galley-style space: dark, closed in, and inadequate to our client's needs. Reinventing it as a minimalist, white-lacquered workspace from Bulthaup helped to lighten up all of the public areas. By tearing down the walls, we were able to include a glossy white island that doubles as a breakfast and cocktail bar. **LEFT:** Atop the breakfast bar, West Coast meets East Coast in a melding of earthy ceramics and sleek urban chic. **RIGHT:** A mid-century étagère holds vintage pottery, including a stylized flower bowl by Gio Ponti. **OPPOSITE:** Once it became clear that our client didn't need a separate formal dining room, we were able to lay out the loft-like portion of his residence. The Saarinen chairs and table feel appropriately light in spirit (and properly mid-century). A collector of photography, he was particularly taken with Daniele Albright's *Species of Space 2*, which can be hung in several different ways. Robert Lewis's chandelier picks up on the branch theme and nods to the industrial elegance of the nearby High Line.

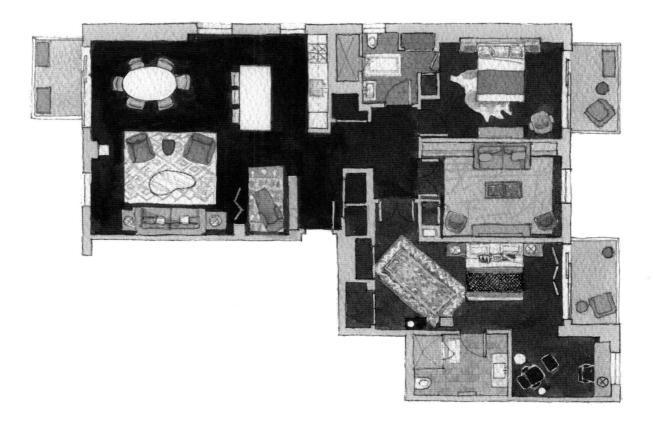

into the dining area and living room. Almost best of all, the reconfiguration yielded another window, and thus more light, in this public zone of the interior.

With spatial relationships and finishes in place, the process of furnishing and accessorizing the rooms with art and objects shifted into high gear. He planned to bring several favorite pieces from his California house: an Eames lounge chair, a persimmon silk quilt, several vintage lamps, a gold sculpture in the shape of a foot that sits atop the "stump" (a petrified-wood side table), the Komar & Melamid piece in the living room, and an oversized urn, a vintage piece of California pottery that introduced the particular shade of orange that repeats in one material or another throughout. For the rest, he wanted mid-century and vintage pieces—and was delighted to search through endless galleries, antiques shops, and boutiques. He also became enamored with one of Brian's paintings that he saw in our office. Now hanging in the reading nook, it set the interior's overall color palette. Many of the furnishings and objects that he found were exceptionally simple, so much so that it required an educated eye to be able to put them into the context of design history. Yet almost all of them have a backstory. More important, they—like this apartment—hold great meaning for him.

OPPOSITE: The den/library can double as an extra bedroom when required. The grasscloth-covered wall of built-ins, rug from Fort Street Studio, and pair of custom wood-and-leather footstools by York Street Studio infuse the room with the earthy, organic materials of which our client is so fond. **ABOVE:** The plan neatly organizes the residence into public and private zones. Among the reasons he purchased this apartment were its several terraces and its proximity to the Hudson River and Hudson River Park.

OPPOSITE: In the master bedroom, a favorite silk quilt brought from California threads the orange color story into the apartment's far reaches; the mid-century rosewood bed is by Robert Baron for Glenn of California. The late Stephen Piscuskas painted the oil hanging over the bed. **ABOVE:** Beside the vintage black lacquer dresser is a mid-century Italian valet chair by Ico & Luisa Parisi for Fratelli Reguitti; its rush seat cleverly conceals a storage compartment.

TOP LEFT AND RIGHT: An early rendering for, and the built reality of, the second bathroom (en suite with the second bedroom), which does double duty as a powder room. **ABOVE LEFT AND RIGHT:** Within the tight confines of the master bath, custom ebonized and mirrored built-ins maximize available storage. The rendering also shows a full-length mirror, devised to cover a mechanical protrusion that we couldn't remove, and the seamless flow of the stone wainscoting and flooring into the glass shower. **OPPOSITE:** With two grown-up children who come and go, the guest bedroom is always at the ready. Norman Cherner's molded-plywood armchair fits neatly in the corner. One of Brian's resin paintings rests on the nightstand; the abstract canvases atop the headboard are by Stephen Pisckuskas.

Architects often talk about the "parti," the defining idea that informs the abstract thinking around a specific project. Since a parti shapes the decision making from conception to completion, from a philosophical perspective it serves as a project's alpha and omega. But it is not everything. Every project also benefits from a well-honed narrative that chronicles the story of the individuals in the architecture and choreography of the garden. Somehow, developing a clear, episodic tale for a property helps to ground its parti in the personal, pragmatic, and practical aspects of a client's desires, dreams, and requirements for everyday living. It also creates a comprehensible framework for testing whether a given design scheme is appropriate or not. If the choice under discussion fits seamlessly into the context of the narrative, then we know to hold on to it until it proves itself intrinsic to the design. If it doesn't, then out it goes.

The epic of house and garden can proceed in myriad ways. Generally, though, the tale begins in the middle of things—the owners' lives, their history with particular houses and gardens, their past experiences with architecture and design—so part of the development process involves research to discover whatever backstory there may be. Some people present that right up front, arriving with stacks of images of places and looks they love that they've collected over the years. The challenge then is to listen hard and look harder in order to distill those images into a compelling and resonant narrative that weaves together lifestyle, architecture, and aesthetic. Suppose a young married couple, living in Manhattan but with an imminent move back to their native California, happens to be enchanted with the great nineteenth- and early twentieth-century estates up and down the Eastern Seaboard. An appropriate design narrative for them might involve a house inspired by the great estates that populated the landscape of Hollywood's Golden Age, either one with the spirit, atmosphere, and details of the kind that F. Scott Fitzgerald described in his fictional West Egg or, perhaps, like those of the fictionalized Long Island property immortalized in Billy Wilder's *Sabrina* (minus the indoor tennis courts; interestingly, Wilder filmed those scenes in one of Los Angeles's great houses, now demolished). The exterior and interior architectural details— windows, doorframes, moldings, baseboards—will all derive from and contribute to that story line. Certain understated flourishes will start to emerge as dominant, enriching the story with texture and embroidering it with specificity. A similar process might result in a different visual outcome for a young family with a passion for the outdoor life and a taste for organic materials and a well-crafted modern style who lives on Manhattan's Upper East Side in rooms graced with classic French proportions but lacking the richness and refinement that beautiful millwork and architectural detailing provide.

The possibilities for plotlines are never ending. Some properties may be pure fantasy insofar as they create (or re-create) an idea of an ideal. These kinds of narratives tend to be tightly focused on a particular, appropriate architectural precedent or vernacular, or perhaps even on an individual architect or historic house. Imagine, for example, a peripatetic couple with a passion for all things French, but especially for Provence and the Côte d'Azur. Significant collectors with a love of antiques, on trip after trip they ship home container loads of acquisitions (including major architectural elements) for their yet-to-be-built dream house. For them, a classic bastide, or farmhouse, from the South of France seems a perfect precedent, and one that's ripe for translation to Southern California. The climates match. The flora isn't all that dissimilar. The farmhouse makes sense in Southern California, where agriculture (and therefore farm dwellings) has long flourished. And the idea of a new French farmhouse constructed from a rigorously studied reinterpretation of a vernacular ideal provides a fitting model for incorporating all their desires—and possessions—in a completely organic way.

When the project involves a renovation of, adaptive reuse for, or addition to an existing property, the authorial challenge shifts in tenor because the visual and conceptual language of the project is already in place. The first set of decisions we make when we're deciding how to move the narrative along has to do with whether (and how) to replicate or reinterpret the established details or depart from them entirely. We are predisposed to carry the past forward, or at least make reference to it, rather than break from it entirely. Whatever the decision, the house always tells the architect how to proceed. And if it's a historic house and the surviving design elements are strong enough, they provide the grammar and syntax for how to proceed.

Because we started our careers in historic renovation and adaptive reuse, and because we love history, our goal is to find the structure and the story beneath the gloss of any detail and puzzle out its how, what, and why. Once we really understand all of that, we can plot the project's overall narrative, chapter by chapter.

NARRATIVE

Into the Woods

LONG-DISTANCE PROJECTS TEND TO PRESENT A PARTICULARLY complex set of design and logistical challenges, especially when they involve family. This five-bedroom New York residence, designed for Raun's brother and his wife just as they were beginning their family (she was expecting twins at the time), is a case in point. Architecture and design rely on clear communication for ultimate success, especially when it's not possible to be on the ground 24/7. Thanks to twenty-first-century technology, we could keep up with each other in ways that wouldn't have been possible years ago.

For this, their first true home, they envisioned a residence that was modern though not minimal (she loves Nakashima), but also inflected with references to nature, as they are both passionate about the outdoors. All that seemed more than possible to achieve in this apartment, given numerous spatial advantages that were ripe for enhancement and fairly straightforward architectural drawbacks that were easily correctible (up to a point). On the plus side, it had well-proportioned rooms with high ceilings and a smartly organized floor plan that required only a few tweaks to clarify the interior relationships. Among its shortcomings were a windowless kitchen, the absence of any architectural detail whatsoever, and a desperate need (as is so often the case in New York) for more storage. In addition, the separation between the public and private areas needed reinforcing.

The effort to infuse the interiors with an architectural presence began at the entry, which lacked definition. In the process of transforming this space so that it could set the stage for what followed, it became the cornerstone and the fulcrum for everything in the apartment. The palette of natural materials began to assert itself here, with wood storage elements establishing character and creating architecture where none existed before. The addition of a much-needed case

PRECEDING PAGES: A multi-paneled resin screen commissioned from Emmanuel Cobbet of Huit 17 brings texture and luminosity to a vertical surface in the dining room; pragmatically, it conceals an oversized air grille. In the corner, a patinated bronze vase sits atop an antique Chinese cabinet from Charles Jacobsen. OPPOSITE: Raun's brother and sister-in-law share a modern aesthetic, an eye for organic materials, and a love of the outdoors. The entry introduces all three with wood elements and a custom case piece with bookshelves and painted doors in thematic, natural hues. ABOVE: They needed storage and the apartment needed architectural distinction, so we used the one to create the other in the entrance to the living room. RIGHT: A carved-wood console from their collection displays a modern lamp and favorite objects, including a set of handmade wood vases collected on their travels to Africa.

ABOVE: In an early rendering for the living room, we established a foundational furniture plan. **BELOW:** In the finished space, an earthy Barkskin wallcovering introduces texture and an elegant, natural note. **RIGHT:** Well-proportioned and light-filled, the living room weaves in some items from their past among carefully selected vintage pieces in the earthy modern style that they love; a John Wigmore light sculpture hangs over the sofa. Sheer wool casement curtains hang like columns, adding definition and rhythm to the interior vista as they filter the light.

ABOVE: An early rendering of the dining room explores an idea for a grid-like screening device with adjustable, curved panels to conceal a massive air grille on one wall. Needless to say, it became the room's focal point, endowing the rather generic room with both decorative layers and architectural rigor. **OPPOSITE:** Because the kitchen lacked a window, we covered one wall with a photo mural to bring in a reference to the outdoors. The leather banquette by York Street Studio provides an earthy contrast to the white resin table and Saarinen chairs.

piece with bookshelves and painted doors introduced the thematic hues of green, brown, and lavender (the palette of the earth needs the colors of the sky for balance). In a sense, the cabinetry became like a canvas.

Two floor-to-ceiling wood storage cabinets to house much of their fine china and tabletop items also contain the A/V equipment; with all the hardware hidden, the arrangement reads as a paneled portal that frames the entrance to the living room. There, sheer wool casement curtains hang in architectural columns at the French doors; with deep borders in a contrasting textile to suggest a wainscot, they frame the view and ground the living room. Textural wall covering, a sophisticated but earthy Barkskin, imbues the space with a sense of nature.

In the dining room, a multipaneled resin screen, custom designed for the space, covers an oversized air grille. Art and architecture both, the screen layers the wall with dimensional, functional elements: the panels can be rotated at will to direct the airflow.

Because they opted against redoing the entire kitchen, it was important to find a way to transform it while leaving an existing leather banquette, cabinets, and stone surfaces in place. The addition of stainless-steel backsplash tiles provided reflectivity. Covering one wall with a mural of a forest in the fall introduced a landscape in lieu of a window.

They had wanted to keep certain pieces of furniture that they loved, so we wove those into the fabric of the design and built the décor around them. Understated patterns, a range of textures, and organic, luxe materials throughout helped layer the rooms with personality and a sense of their own developing history.

The large, wood-framed armoire reiterates the grid expressed elsewhere in the apartment; incorporated into one wall of the master bedroom, it conceals a closet. The chest of drawers, bench, and bed further the earthy, organic aesthetic. Nancy Lorenz's multimedia painting (including mother-of-pearl) over the bed, the polished marble top of the Saarinen side table, and a silk carpet soften the elemental, even rugged pieces with grace notes of reflectivity and shimmer.

More than any other elements of architecture, interiors, and landscape design, light and color define character and sense of place. So we obsess over each design decision because every choice we make, no matter how seemingly trivial, affects the nature and quality of the atmosphere and mood that light and color create throughout the house and its outdoor spaces. How does the structure make its connection to natural light? How does that light permeate into a particular interior recess or garden area? What kind of reflections does it create off, and through, windows, walls, or water? How does illumination change to shadow over the course of the day? In what ways does that transition from day to night affect the color palette within the room and in the garden? How do volumes, furnishings, materials, and objects—inside and outside—appear in natural, man-made, and both types of illumination from dawn to dusk? What cues from nature might prompt the palette of materials and finishes within and without: pale to dark, cool to warm, ethereal to saturated? What effect do the chosen surfaces and their respective finishes have? Where should matte shift to glossy, and back again? What are the best options for choreographing the flow of illumination and color palette to maximize habitability and happiness? What is the best way to weave the elements of tone, hue, and finish through the interior and exterior to tie all the spaces together, however boldly or quietly? All these concerns and many others have an impact on the quality of luminosity, the perception and effect of color, and the feeling of physical comfort achieved within the given surroundings.

The orientation of the house to the exterior is a priority of ours that stems from more than just an idea about the proper physical relationship between inside and outside, house and garden, room and view. The way we position a house quite literally allows us to build light and an array of hues into the structure. It also involves far more than just providing direct vistas into the outdoor rooms and gardens. We always look for ways to frame apertures to capture a high horizon line or a tree, a mountain peak in the far distance, a stand of grasses or hedges in the mid-range, a profusion of flowers or succulents nearby. We often try to add a source of natural light from above in order to enhance the quality of light and array of shades and tones within the interiors (everything from the choice of wall paint to trim finishes, from flooring to counters to furnishings). Light wells, skylights, mirrors, and more can work their magic in so many different ways to create a kaleidoscopic evolution of effects from day to night, from one season to the next.

In the landscape, the spectacular range of hues in light, plant life, and geology are among nature's great atmospheric wonders. Yet it's always possible to find ways to use design consciously to create conditions that modulate or subtly enhance the existing effects. Certain plantings, for example, may feel optimal for a particular location in a garden or landscape partly because the placement and selection of hues provides interest and focus up close, and a seemingly integral transition to or barrier from the space beyond. The specific shape and arrangement of branches and leaves may filter the rays of the sun like a stencil into a pattern that may be especially appropriate in form to the context and interiors of that particular house. The same can be said of the color palette, for one can compose a landscape as a canvas with impasto brushstrokes of plant life and the accompanying elements of hardscape, down to the planters and pots. The evolving play of light and shadow set in motion by the forms and tonal counterpoint of foliage generates a fade-in/fade-out drama all its own throughout the day. And the way that water reflects and refracts light into color? Yes, that is pure physics. But such optical effects can, and often do, endlessly enchant the eye from dawn to dusk and into the night. As for the addition of night lighting in the landscape? That creates layers of drama that resolve, and dissolve, into nature's storied depths of darkness.

Design is in many ways a matter of physical and emotional punctuation, establishing a unique but necessary rhythm to daily life through the variety of shaped experiences: the size of individual volumes, the balance of proportions from one room to the next, the placement of windows and framing of views, the articulation and decoration of the interior and the exterior space. Not every room should be the same size or have the same level of light, much less the same palette. And not every room needs to explode with light and color, always. There is such a thing as too much of a much-ness: we need our cozy rooms for their intimacy, just as we love our grand ones for their expansiveness.

When a place has a certain quality of air, color, and light—and gives clear clues about how to inhabit it—it has the corporeal effect of inducing physical and emotional comfort. A light-washed house amid gardens with shady spots, variegated greenery, differentiated textures and materials, visible paths, conscious introduction of particular hues, and distinctive destinations is welcoming by definition. This type of place can exist in any style, for the fundamental assumptions that drive its design have nothing to do with style. The core attributes of such realms begin with trying to weave together inside and outside. And in the consonance between the two, the character of that place emerges.

LIGHT *and* COLOR

The French Connection

AVID FRANCOPHILES, THIS COUPLE FIRST CAME TO US IN THE MID-1990s to create a French-inspired garden on their five-acre lot in Rancho Santa Fe. In sketch after sketch, a series of rather grand, typically Gallic gestures began to take shape: long axial views up the gentle hill at the property's rear, a half-acre pond at the property's lower end, and the characteristic, elegant unfolding of lawns, pavilions, and fountains, all framed by a perimeter of hedges, trees, salvaged palms, and more. Working through the project in the drawings also helped to clarify specific ideas of how the garden would look over time, in five-year increments, as it grew to

PRECEDING PAGES: A custom wrought-iron gate opens onto an ultra-lush, drought-resistant garden with eucalyptus, California pepper trees, Canary Island date palms, and sycamores—a Southern California dream of southern France. **ABOVE:** From the moment these clients commissioned us to build this house, we imagined it as a bastide. **LEFT:** The front façade evolved through the planning stages into a more compact massing but kept the essence of its character as originally conceived. **BELOW:** The design of the gardens preceded the design of the house, so the long axis through the property was already well established by the time we began to site the structures. **OPPOSITE TOP:** Through the parking court's antique gates, the choreography of entrance offers a first glimpse of the front façade and main entry. **OPPOSITE BOTTOM:** In the latest re-envisioning of the gardens, we introduced a stone stair, with risers of hand-chiseled Moroccan zellige tiles, that cascades down to the newly drought-tolerant gardens around the pond opposite the main façade.

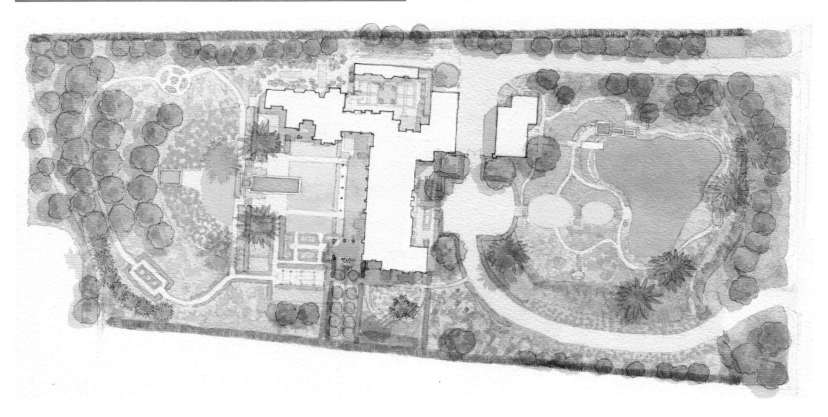

full maturity. So when they later asked us to design a house based on a bastide, the iconic farmhouse form of Provence, its form truly emerged from the garden.

So many projects come to us as a family is moving from one phase of life into another. That was true in this case. The last of three children was just about to leave home. The couple's first grandchild had just been born. They envisioned this home not only as a gathering place for their family but also as their own private retreat. By this time, they had been collecting antique furnishings, objects, and architectural elements in France for more than a decade. They continued to travel during the design and construction phases of the project. In all, they must have shipped back forty containers' worth of antique floors, windows, eighteenth-century boiserie rooms, fireplaces, pavers, and roofing from France (their roof tiles, which predate those of the local Spanish mission, may be the oldest construction elements in San Diego County). The puzzle became how and where to enfold a raft of specific items organically into the structure and furnishings of the house and garden. In the conscious weaving together of old and new components, the French treasures took pride of place in the specific areas they sparked into being. That was the beginning.

Nearly two decades and many projects later, the couple decided they wanted to move on from this house to something simpler. They entertained the idea of building a new house— and after much discussion, jettisoned it. Instead, a collective decision emerged to reconceive the existing house. In so doing, a reinvention of the property occurred. The result? They "fell in love with the house all over again."

Once more we started with the gardens. Part of the objective was to address California's new normal of less is more where water usage is concerned. These had never been incredibly thirsty gardens, but removing more than three-quarters of the existing lawns reduced their water consumption dramatically.

To have the opportunity to return to a fully matured landscape and refine its lower reaches—the shrubbery and more ephemeral plantings—that is a garden designer's dream. In the broadest terms, this latest reset of the landscape reinvented the way the garden should look now and going forward within its existing, scrim-like outer perimeter of adult trees. We retained the original orientation, all the major elements, and the mature trees while finessing the detailing and size of the beds, the organization and layering of the plantings within those beds, and the conception of some of the pathways and courtyards. The grand scheme offered the opportunity to clarify the grading, reduce the size of the upper lawn, and, in the spirit of Le Nôtre, slope and align the existing axis perfectly in the view. In the side gardens, grass and thirsty plants gave way to gravel and carpets of pavers and stones, with a little inspiration from Nicole de Vésian. All of the reorganization occurred within an equally formal French plan, but with a very exotic succulent palette that created an almost lapidary garden. The overall effect is spatially similar, yet even more redolent of its inspirations.

ABOVE LEFT: The window and door placement creates a rhythmic flow of light into the entry hall, where a floor of French limestone in a classic cabochon pattern with inset squares of black stone sets the stage. Atop the console hangs an eighteenth-century painted panel. **ABOVE RIGHT:** One of the gems in the couple's collection of antique French architectural elements was this wrought-iron balustrade; we designed the entry hall stair to fit its full length and sweep. **OPPOSITE:** Demarcated by a change to French parquet de Versailles flooring, the interior public rooms unfold off the foyer in an enfilade, creating a grand view of the layering of space from one end the house to the other.

A similar transformation happened with the interiors. The goal of the redesign was to liven up the rooms, to make them more current and less formal. This we did—room by room—by breaking out of the eighteenth century while retaining, repositioning, and regrouping their extensive collections of French furnishings, art, and objects. Some aspects of this undertaking proved to be a graphic puzzle. Some were structural. Some depended on color. All depended on function.

The grandly proportioned living room, the house's center point, had long had an appropriate formality—all symmetry, taffeta, buttons, and antique trims. But, though beautifully furnished with French antiques, it lacked seating scaled for the twentieth or twenty-first centuries, so it was far less inviting than it should have been. In terms of décor, the task was to retain the room's architectural grandeur but enhance its comfort and functionality.

First came the furniture plan. Then came the paint, an ultra-sophisticated shade of pink that we keyed to a particular hue in the sky of a pair of Barbizon School paintings that have pride of place in the room. With grayed moldings and deep aubergine–lacquered doors, the interior envelope sparked to life. Having solved the color puzzle, we reupholstered the newly selected furnishings scavenged from their other properties, storage rooms, and other parts of the house in a palette derived from the paintings. The sense of welcome is palpable and still very, very French.

Inspired by the bar at the Hotel Ritz in Paris, their barroom, paneled in boiserie, opens off the living room. It, too, needed a reset. Lacquering the boiserie in blue-gray and installing mirrors in the paneling over the seating area helped light to dance through the space. A period French stone fireplace, part of the original interior, served as inspiration for the room's new palette of red, greige, black, and gray. A gray, 1920s-style carpet with aubergine accents introduced interesting notes of contrast. The library, a separate boiserie-paneled space just opposite the bar, also underwent a makeover: the décor now centers around a Picasso tapestry purchased on a recent trip to Paris.

LEFT: In its most recent redesign, the boiserie-paneled family room/library has relaxed into an open, welcoming contemporaneity. To recast the room in this lighter, yet still elegant, mood, we rearranged the existing furniture to improve the internal flow and better suit the palette of the Picasso-designed tapestry that hangs so prominently (dating to the 1950s, it is based on his 1911 painting *Le pigeon aux petit pois*).
ABOVE: In a nod to the legendary French decorator Henri Samuel, the tapestry is hung atop the boiserie.

LEFT: In their glamorous formal living room, this couple's Francophilia reaches one of its many joyful apotheoses. Over the sofa hangs one of a pair of Barbizon School paintings, which suggested the color palette and anchor the room. **ABOVE:** Longtime collectors, they brought home a bust of Marie Antoinette, who adds her feminine air to the mantel, from one of their many trips. **BELOW LEFT:** The furniture plan reiterates that symmetry of pairings, with fraternal-twin seating groups (same arrangements, different yet related pieces) acting as parentheses to a central conversational array focused on the antique stone fireplace. **BELOW RIGHT:** A gilded French starburst mirror draws the eye to Marcellin Desboutin's 1897 self-portrait. **OPPOSITE:** In the spirit of the mix, modern forms, patterns, and textures create a harmonious counterpoint to the room's eighteenth-century paintings and porcelains. The carpet provided the foundation for the color palette. The Maison Jansen coffee table is a find from a trip to Paris.

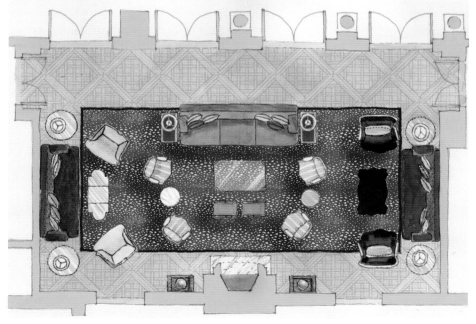

The very ornate dining room had always had a Marie Antoinette quality. To bring it up to date without losing its distinctive *je ne sais quoi*, we reinvented its palette in shades of pale gray, black, and gold. With reupholstered seating, the couple's finest pair of eighteenth-century sideboards, pieces from their alabaster collection, and ormolu candelabra, it sings with glamour. A painting commissioned from Brian especially for the space took the place of an antique French cartoon.

One of the few true structural amendments involved the addition of steel-framed glass doors to enclose an outdoor loggia that links the kitchen to the guesthouse. Centered on a large refectory table (a longtime favorite piece), new woven chairs, and an outdoor carpet, this space became an informal dining room that has an outdoor feeling—and that they now use all the time. A bit more reconfiguring and the addition of sofas scaled for the twenty-first century transformed the adjacent guesthouse living room into a family room where they happily watch TV and read.

Through the years and successive iterations, this property has developed its own sense of history. It gave us great pleasure to reinvent it for their next phase by finding a way to help them see anew the collected pieces that they care for most.

OPPOSITE: The boiserie-lined barroom was inspired by the bar at Le Bristol Hotel in Paris. **ABOVE:** Newly lacquered in an evanescent shade of blue-gray, selected to complement the veining in the marble bar counter and antique mantelpiece, the woodwork seems practically to dissolve in the light. The addition of mirror on the wall over the sofa encourages the reflections to dance through the space. Vintage gilded French stools and a vintage Sabino ceiling fixture provide additional layers of history.

OPPOSITE: To give the formal dining room a twenty-first-century flair while retaining many of its eighteenth-century inflections, we recast the palette in gold, black, and an ultra-pale blue-gray. Commissioned for the spot (and replacing an eighteenth-century cartoon), one of Brian's multi-paneled paintings in ink, encaustic, and gold leaf swirls above one of the couple's finest pair of eighteenth-century sideboards (its mate is on the opposite wall). **ABOVE:** Alabaster and ormolu pieces from their collections draw the eye to the room's fine details. **OVERLEAF LEFT:** A tapestry of succulents, including *Senecio*, aloe, and agave, flourishes in the garden off the studio. **TOP RIGHT:** Little Ollies border an outdoor dining area under a trellised bower of climbing roses, which offer shade, perfume, and a romantic atmosphere. **CENTER RIGHT:** Redesigned during California's severe drought, this hidden side-yard garden now features an allée of dwarf St. Mary's magnolia trees divided by a stone rill set in gravel. **BOTTOM RIGHT:** Also re-landscaped in response to the drought, gardens surrounding the pool retain their original, Le Nôtre-inspired formal plan, extended vista, and controlled horizon line. Now, however, a border of *Salvia leucantha* 'Santa Barbara' (Mexican bush sage) embraces a much-reduced, demilune-shaped lawn.

TOP: By enclosing an outdoor dining loggia adjacent to the kitchen with steel-framed windows and doors, we transformed an occasionally used casual dining area into an everyday destination. **ABOVE:** The house's French country design DNA was already apparent in our earliest concepts for the kitchen. **OPPOSITE:** Even from the kitchen's hardest-working areas the views are captivating. **OVERLEAF:** With its vintage French garden furniture and glazed Provençal garden containers, all shaded by a canopy of wisteria that climbs a painted-steel trellis, this area just outside the living room offers a taste of the South of France in California.

ABOVE LEFT AND RIGHT: The gardens of Nicole de Vesian inspired the drought-tolerant reinvention of this former green space into a gravel courtyard with a strategically placed, shell-shaped wall fountain and plantings of coast rosemary. The rendering served to explain de Vesian's considered use of topiaries for visual punctuation. **BELOW LEFT:** In the walled kitchen courtyard garden, a newly installed eighteenth-century Portuguese tiled panel adorns this tiny covered nook, creating a focal point—and a "secret" sitting area for the grandchildren. **BELOW CENTER:** An antique terra-cotta French olive jar and agaves planted in glazed antique Provençal urns stand out against the stone-and-plaster kitchen courtyard wall. **BELOW RIGHT:** Designed and built specifically for the location, this stone fountain also incorporates the clients' antique tiles. **OPPOSITE:** In response to the drought, the former lawned area off the kitchen became a dry, gravel garden. The paving grid incorporates the clients' antique French stone tiles. Boston ivy curtains the upper reaches of the house with color and texture.

ABOVE AND BELOW: Her closet and dressing area incorporate favorite pieces brought back from France, including cabinets designed and made for Le Meurice Hotel in Paris, which we painted a glossy pale lavender; newly added mirrors in their upper panels help reflect light around the room. **RIGHT:** The master bedroom includes many of the couple's furniture finds from the French flea market.

OPPOSITE: The millwork in his closet is as precisely detailed, organized, and compartmentalized as in a haberdashery. The painting, by Philippe Conrad, dates to the 1950s. ABOVE: The marble washstand in a ground-floor powder room off the entry enfilade rests atop a French antique iron base. The overdoor is also French antique ironwork.

ABOVE AND OPPOSITE: Reinventing the guesthouse living room as a family room for the main house has given the couple another favorite gathering place. The antique panels of painted boiserie hail most recently from Andy Warhol's Paris apartment and provide a backdrop for the vintage French club chairs (still dressed in their original red leather). Two mirrored wood panels flank the window bay. Painted-wood consoles display some of the couple's extensive collection of blue-and-white porcelains. An antique panel over the door adds a final flourish.

ABOVE: In the "Green Room" of the guesthouse, we refreshed the upholstered scroll bed with a geometric printed linen by Peter Dunham. The antique tallboy draws focus upward to the beamed ceiling. **OPPOSITE:** A guest room with a view, the Green Room overlooks a terrace furnished for alfresco dining. *Aeoniums* in terra-cotta pots bring the garden right up to the windowsill.

LEFT AND ABOVE: For an update on a classic French country look, we re-covered the walls of this guesthouse bedroom in a Manuel Canovas toile with a palette that complements the painted ceiling beams. Chamfered mirrors reflect the wallcovering's charming rural scenes—and the gardens beyond the windows.

OPPOSITE: Meandering pathways connect the house, the studio, and the pond. From the outset, the plan for the new succulent garden included various species of *Aeonium*, *Cotyledon*, *Crassula*, *Senecio*, *Sedum*, and *Euphorbia*. **ABOVE:** California pepper trees overhang the water garden with its stepped cascade of connecting pools. **RIGHT:** Early study drawing for the water garden terrace.

ABOVE, LEFT TO RIGHT: Now rooted, the array of succulents mingles as originally planned: two types of agave, *Aeonium* 'Mint Saucer', and *Senecio serpens*; *Agave americana* 'Marginata'; *Aloe vera* and *Aeonium* 'Jack Catlin'. **BELOW, LEFT TO RIGHT:** *Agave attenuata* and *Senecio mandraliscae*; a mix of *Aeoniums* and *Cistanthe grandiflora*. **OPPOSITE:** To provide a focal point, a terra-cotta urn terminates the axis of this gravel path bordered by *Westringia* and roses. **OVERLEAF:** A majestic pair of Canary Island palms bracket the rear façade of the house and stake out defining perimeter points for the view. In the foreground are *Salvia leucantha* 'Santa Barbara' (Mexican bush sage); a hedge of *Olea europaea* 'Montra' (dwarf olive) backs up to the pool.

Climate is intrinsic to defining the essence of place—and therefore to the architectural expression of the type of relationship between indoors and outdoors. In whatever region we work, we consciously factor this issue of transition into our design plan. California, for example, enjoys an unusually amorphous edge between inside and outside. From a design perspective, that allows the house and the garden to bleed into each other organically. Regardless of location, however, it is important to tie the interior and exterior together as fully and beautifully as possible. This involves more than simply using the obvious building elements—windows and French doors, for example—to encourage views and easy communication between the enclosed and open environments. It requires conceptualizing the property as a whole, and programming the interior and exterior simultaneously whenever possible.

Envisioning the design of the living landscape together with its fixed structural components affects the way we shape the house and its rooms because what the house looks out to is integral to its orientation, plan, and detailing. We may sketch out the plant palette even before the idea of the house begins to materialize in any real way. This approach allows us to take a client's color preferences, sense of form, and interest in pattern into account from the outset, all of which will make a difference in how the house ultimately feels when it is built and decorated. On occasion, these considerations also affect the footprint of the house. Sometimes a building that is smaller than desired actually serves those who will live in it better because, by allowing more adjacent space for gardens, and more expansive views of them, it affords more opportunity to bring the outside in. On the other hand, reducing the size of the structure can present challenges for some of the rooms and also raises the corollary issue of whether each activity requires a separate room. Perhaps one or more multipurpose rooms might be preferable, as spaces that accommodate more than one pursuit tend to add the layers of meaning that will make the rooms richer in the end.

INSIDE/OUTSIDE

Conceptualizing beautifully proportioned gardens before conceiving beautifully proportioned rooms heightens the opportunity to utilize all of the space on the property from lot line to core with grace and economy. We are always thinking about the possibilities that are inherent in the exterior. Where can the gardens be? How can we weave the near, mid-range, and far views into the fabric of the building and its interiors? How best can we create space outside that then communicates with the inside?

The choreography of the flow between and through indoors and outdoors follows an inherent logic of relationships. A kitchen, for example, should open easily to an outside dining area or exterior living space around a fireplace or water feature whenever possible and practical. Sometimes it makes sense to relate the indoor and outdoor spaces especially closely through materials and color palettes that reflect, complement, or extend those of the plantings and exterior hardscape; in this way, any boundaries between the two blur or disappear altogether. On other occasions it is possible to expand the overall living space by appropriating parts of the exterior at a farther remove from the house and transforming them into outdoor rooms. Landscapes feel—and become—habitable when they unfold with clearly defined destinations and places to sit. Establishing a sense of enclosure through hedges, fencing, or some other type of framing element accomplishes that goal elegantly, with the added benefit that the vertical components become part of the garden's structural reality.

If the spatial quality of inside and outside as a unified whole is our primary consideration, the style of the two runs a very close second. That decision is personal to each homeowner. Even so, context plays a significant role in the eventual choice, as some styles and design vocabularies are more appropriate in certain settings than others. Always, the house and its surroundings are harmoniously in synch, if not literally a stylistic match. Though we may pair the English inspired with English inspired, the range of the precedents can span the reach of the one-time British Empire. A similar breadth adheres to the French tradition, and to the Mediterranean and Moorish as well. And always, the visual language reflects who the occupants are, how they live, and the surrounding context. What do they really want in their house? In what ways and how should the interior reflect the exterior? How public and/or private do they wish to be? In what ways do they want to inhabit the outside? The answers to these questions and more start to dictate how an overall design and its various components interact with the reality of the site. Every house should have places indoors and out that speak to the specific needs and desires of its occupants. Once those parameters become clear, it is then possible to plan an appropriate way for the interior of the house to lay out with apposite and fitting exterior spaces.

Conceiving a unified vision for the property as a whole extends to the smallest details of the interior architecture and, when the opportunity presents itself, to selecting materials, color palettes, furnishings, textiles, and other elements of décor. As architects, we are always responsible for the interior architecture, even when there is a collaborating interior designer. On occasion, in addition to designing the house and its surroundings, we may also handle the interior design and decoration. Always, we work closely with the owners and any other members of the design team to incorporate their visions into the place we are all creating together. We revel in the privilege of bringing interior and exterior into play simultaneously. Our goal is to knit them together seamlessly. When that happens, the spatial experience can be extraordinary.

Sources

OUTSIDE

LANDSCAPE INSTALLERS

Clark and White Landscape
clarkandwhitelandscape.com

Golden Leaf Landscape Care
goldenleaflandscape.com

Landscape Discoveries
landscapediscoveries.com

NURSERIES AND GARDEN SUPPLIERS

C&S Nursery
csnursery.com

Eye of the Day Garden Design Center
eyeofthedaygdc.com

Forrest Keeling Nursery
fknursery.com

Fox Point Farms
foxpointfarms.com

The Gardener
thegardener.com

Hashimoto Nursery
hashimotonursery.com

Le Prince Jardinier
princejardinier.fr/en/

Marina del Rey Garden Center
marinagardencenter.com

Native Sons
nativeson.com

Roger's Gardens
rogersgardens.com

Rolling Greens
rollinggreensnursery.com

Root Pouch
rootpouch.com

San Marcos Growers
smgrowers.com

Suncrest Nurseries Inc.
suncrestnurseries.com

Theodore Payne Foundation for Wild Flowers and Native Plants
theodorepayne.org

Van Engelen
vanengelen.com

OUTDOOR CUSTOM UPHOLSTERY AND AWNINGS

Awnings of Distinction by Marine Awnings Co.
awningsofdistinction.com

OUTDOOR FURNITURE, GARDEN ACCESSORIES, AND ORNAMENT

Barbara Israel
barbaraisrael.com

Berbere World Imports
berbereworldimports.com

Charles Jacobsen
charlesjacobsen.com

David Sutherland
davidsutherlandshowroom.com

Formations
formationsusa.com

Hervé Baume
herve-baume.com

Inner Gardens
innergardens.com

Intérieurs
interieurs.com

Jalan Jalan Imports
jalanjalanimports.com

Janus et Cie
janusetcie.com

Kenneth Lynch & Sons
klynchandsons.com

Marston & Langinger
marstonandlanginger.com

McKinnon and Harris
mckinnonharris.com

Mecox Gardens
mecox.com

Michael Taylor Collection
michaeltaylordesigns.com

Munder Skiles
munder-skiles.com

Santa Barbara Designs
sbumbrella.com

Singh Imports
singhimports.com

Summit
summitfurniture.com

William Laman
williamlaman.com

OUTDOOR LIGHTING

Lantern Masters, Inc.
lanternmasters.com

Luminous Gardens
luminousgardens.com

SPJ Lighting, Inc.
spjlighting.com

Steve Handelman Studios
stevenhandelmanstudios.com

OUTDOOR STONE AND TILE

Bourget Bros.
bourgetbros.com

OUTSIDE/INSIDE

ARCHITECTURAL SPECIALTIES

Cellarworks, Inc. (wine cellars)
cellarworks.com

De Botello Wine Systems (wine cellar racks)
customwineracking.com

Emmanuel Cobbet (resin screens)
huit17.com

Forno Bravo (pizza ovens)
Fornobravo.com

Metal by Kevin (fireplace screens)
metalbykevin.com

Whit McCleod (wine barrel–end flooring)
custommade.com/reclaimed-hex-wine-barrel-end-flooring-2/by/whitmcleodfurniture/

CABINETRY, MILLWORK, AND ORNAMENTAL MOLDINGS

Bulthaup
bulthaup.com

Chesney's (mantels)
chesneys.com

Classical Building Arts, Inc.
(decorative moldings)
classicalbarts.com

Decorators Supply
decoratorssupply.com

Fischer & Jirouch Co. (decorative moldings)
fischerandjirouch.com

Ideal Cabinets
idealcabinets.com

CONTRACTORS

Capstone Construction & Management, Inc.
capstoneconstruct.com

Courtney Construction, Inc.
courtneyconstructioninc.com

Dalton Construction
(323) 654-5051

Eastlake Pools & Landscape Inc.
(818) 881-2150

Emilio & Sons
(858) 561-5820

Franco Restoration Corp.
francorestoration.com

Heltzer Development Group, Inc.
heltzerdev.com

HJH Construction Inc.
(760) 324-0065

RLJ Construction Corporation
(949) 276-2874

DECORATIVE PAINTERS

Dana Westring
callowayart.com/gallery/
contemporary-art/dana-westring

FABRICS AND TRIMS

Clarence House
clarencehouse.com

Cowtan & Tout
cowtan.com

Donghia
donghia.com

John Robshaw Textiles
johnrobshaw.com

Keith McCoy
(310) 657-7150

Kneedler|Fauchère
kneedlerfauchere.com

Lee Jofa
leejofa.com

Nomi Fabrics
nomiinc.com

Opuzen
opuzen.com

Perennials
perennialsfabrics.com

Raoul Textiles
raoultextiles.com

Samuel & Sons
samuelandsons.com

Schumacher
fschumacher.com

Sunbrella
sunbrella.com

HARDWARE

Crown City Hardware
restoration.com

J. Nicolas Architectural Imported Hardware
jnicolas.com

Liz's Antique Hardware
lahardware.com

P.E. Guerin
peguerin.com

Rocky Mountain Hardware
rockymountainhardware.com

Specialty Hardware + Plumbing
specialtyhardware.net

Whitechapel Ltd.
whitechapel-ltd.com

York Street Studio (hardware, leather tiles, furniture, lighting)
yorkstreet.com

LIGHTING

Charles Edwards
charlesedwards.com

Circa Lighting
circalighting.com

Dennis & Leen
dennisandleen.com

Elkhorn Industries, Inc.
flatcreekcrossing.com

Jackson Moore Lighting & Fans
jacksonmoore.com

John Wigmore Light Sculptures
johnwigmore.com

Lost City Arts
lostcityarts.com

Niche Modern
nichemodern.com

Paul Ferrante
paulferrante.com

Remains Lighting
remains.com

Rewire
rewirela.com

Rosemarie Allaire Lighting Design
rald.us/cdm_residence.html

Urban Archaeology
urbanarchaeology.com

The Urban Electric Co.
urbanelectricco.com

Vaughan Designs
vaughandesigns.com

PAINT MANUFACTURERS AND CONTRACTORS

Farrow & Ball
us.farrow-ball.com

Steve Beattie Painting
(310) 476-1947

Sydney Harbour Paint Company
shpcompany.com

PLUMBING

Diamond Spas
diamondspas.com

Dornbracht
dornbracht.com

Hydro Systems
hydrosystem.com

Newport Brass
newportbrass.com

Sonoma Forge
sonomaforge.com

Waterworks
waterworks.com

STONE AND TILE

Ann Sacks
annsacks.com

Caesarstone
caesarstone.com

Carocim
carocim.com

Compas
compasstone.com

Exquisite Surfaces
xsurfaces.com

Lascaux Tile Company
lascauxtile.net

SMG Stone Company
smgstone.com

Waterworks LA
waterworks.com

STRUCTURAL ENGINEERS

Gordon L. Polon Structural
Engineering
gordonpolon.com

Parker Resnick Structural Engineering
parkerresnick.com

WINDOWS AND DOORS

Architectural Iron Works
aiwslo.com

B & B Doors & Windows
(818) 837-8480

Lemar Hardwood & Door Company
lemarhardwood.com

WOOD FLOORING

Carlisle Wide Plank Floors
wideplankflooring.com

DuChâteau
duchateau.com

INSIDE

BOOKSELLERS AND CUSTOM LIBRARIES

Arcana Books on the Arts
arcanabooks.com

The Book Den
bookden.com

Book Soup
booksoup.com

Chevalier's Books
chevaliersbooks.com

Douglas Woods
private.library@icloud.com

Hennessey + Ingalls
hennesseyingalls.com

Jackson Hole Book Traders
(307) 734-6001

Juniper Books
juniperbooks.com

Rizzoli
rizzolibookstore.com

Valley Bookstore
valleybookstore.com

Vromans Bookstore
vromansbookstore.com

William Stout Architectural Books
stoutbooks.com

CLOSETS

The Closet Lady
closetlady.com

Spacemaster Closets, Inc.
(914) 376-1800

CUSTOM UPHOLSTERY

Custom Craft Upholsterers, Inc.
customcraftuph.com

Interiors Haberdashery, LLC
(203) 969-7227

FLOOR COVERINGS

Flor
flor.com

Fort Street Studio
fortstreetstudio.com

Madeline Weinrib
madelineweinrib.com

Mansour Modern
mansourmodern.com

The Rug Company
therugcompany.com

Russell Johnson Imports
russelljohnsonimports.com

Stark
starkcarpet.com

FURNISHINGS AND HOME ACCESSORIES

A. Rudin
arudin.com

ABC Carpet & Home
abchome.com

Ann-Morris
ann-morris.com

Anthropologie
anthropologie.com

Antiqueria Tribeca
Antiqueria.com

Baker Knapp & Tubbs
bakerfurniture.com

Barneys New York
barneys.com

BDDW
bddw.com

Bergdorf Goodman
bergdorfgoodman.com

Blackman Cruz
blackmancruz.com

Blu Dot
bludot.com

Calypso St. Barth
calypsostbarth.com

Carol Gratale
carolegratale.com

CB2
cb2.com

Cisco Home
ciscohome.net

Crate & Barrel
crateandbarrel.com

David Alan
thedavidalancollection.com

De La Espada
delaespada.com

Demisch Danant
demischdanant.com

Design Within Reach, Inc.
dwr.com

Desiron
desiron.com

De Vera Objects
deveraobjects.com

Dragonette
dragonetteltd.com

Duane
duanemodern.com

Dune
dune-ny.com

Fat Chance Los Angeles
(323) 930-1960

1stdibs
1stdibs.com

Fisher Weisman Collection
fisherweisman.com/collection

George Champion Modern Shop
championmodern.com

George Smith
georgesmith.com

Gracious Home New York
gracioushome.com

Gregorius Pineo
gregoriuspineo.com

Herman Miller
hermanmiller.com

Hollyhock
hollyhockinc.com

Holly Hunt
hollyhunt.com

Hollywood at Home
Hollywoodathome.com

Home Again
homeagainjackson.com

Homer
homerdesign.com

Hudson Furniture
hudsonfurnitureinc.com

Jackson Mercantile
jacksonholetraveler.com/profile/
jackson-mercantile

Jayson Home
jaysonhome.com

Jean de Merry
jeandemerry.com

Jonathan Adler
jonathanadler.com

Knoll
knoll.com

Lawson-Fenning
lawsonfenning.com

Lobel Modern NYC
lobelmodern.com

MADE
madejacksonhole.com

Mitchell Gold + Bob Williams
mgbwhome.com

Nancy Corzine
nancycorzine.com

Nathan Turner
nathanturner.com

Oly Studio
olystudio.com

Orange
orangefurniture.com

Paul Marra Design
paulmarradesign.com

Plantation
plantationdesign.com

Pottery Barn
potterybarn.com

Ralph Lauren Home
ralphlauren.com

Ralph Pucci
ralphpucci.net

Restoration Hardware
restorationhardware.com

Robert Lewis Studio
robertlewisstudio.com

Room & Board
roomandboard.com

Ruzzetti & Gow
creelandgow.com

Serena & Lily
serenaandlily.com

Simon Pearce
simonpearce.com

Thomas Hayes Studio
thomashayesstudio.com

Thomas Lavin
thomaslavin.com

TROY
(212) 941-4777

Twentieth
twentieth.net

Twenty Two | Home
twentytwohome.com

Valley Drapery & Upholstery
valleydrapery.com

West Elm
westelm.com

Williams Sonoma Home
williams-sonoma.com

Worlds Away
worlds-away.com

Wyeth
wyeth.nyc

GALLERIES, ART CONSULTANTS, AND FINE ART FRAMERS/INSTALLERS

Alan Moss
1stdibs.com/dealers/alan-moss

Artistic Frame
artisticframe.com

Cadogan Tate
cadogantate.com

Crown Point Press
crownpoint.com

David Storey
studiostorey@gmail.com

Diehl Gallery
diehlgallery.com

Gallery BAC
gallerybac.com

Gemini G.E.L.
geminigel.com

L.A. Louver
lalouver.com

Teton Art Services
tetonartservices.com

INTERIOR DESIGNERS

Thomas M. Beeton (art consulting and interior design)
beetonassociates.com

John Cottrell Co.
(310) 247-1355

Fisher Weisman
Fisherweisman.com

Suzanne Rheinstein
suzannerheinstein.com

Madeline Stuart
madelinestuart.com

Kelly Wearstler
Kellywearstler.com

INSTALLATION/MOVING/ DELIVERIES

AAA Packing and Shipping, Inc.
aaapack.com

Bevard Delivery
(323) 653-2273

Black Diamond Moving and Storage
blackdiamondmoving.com

CR Creative Services
crcreativeservices.com

LINENS AND ACCESSORIES

Anichini
anichini.com

Frette
frette.com

Jackson Hole Pendleton
indianblanket.com

Linen Alley
linenalley.com

Matteo
matteohome.com

Pratesi
pratesi.com

Quilts of Gee's Bend
1stdibs.com

WALL COVERINGS

Caba Company
barkskin.com

Cole & Son
cole-and-son.com/en/

Maya Romanoff
www.mayaromanoff.com

Rick Wooldridge Wallcovering
rickwooldridge.com

Roger Arlington
rogerarlington.com

Wolf Gordon
wolf-gordon.com

WINDOW TREATMENTS

Aero Shade
aeroshadeco.com

Architectural Window Shades
awshades.com

Creative Draperies of California
cdoc4u.com

Le Décor Français
(212) 734-0032

Marcia Levine – The Workroom
(917) 446-2154

Willow Creek Home Furnishings
willowcreekhf.com

*For Ava, with love and gratitude, especially for
tolerating her parents' incessant talk about architecture
and gardens for the past two decades*

Acknowledgments

This book, and the body of work it represents, would not have been possible without the support and collaborative efforts of many people, too many, in fact, to name individually. We have had the good fortune to be a part of families who have encouraged our work from the start, no matter how eccentric our course may have seemed at times. We are deeply grateful to our siblings—Karen and Jeff Thorp, Jay Tichenor, and Kary Nelson—who allowed us to advise them and even work on their houses and gardens. Special thanks to Jeff and his wife, Lisa, who trusted us to help them create their first family apartment in New York and were willing to take another chance and let us design their Western dream house. A boundless debt of gratitude is owed to our parents, from whom we learned so much: Dody and Don Tichenor, who were always building something, and Vivian and Edward Thorp, who entrusted us with the design of their house and garden on their magnificent property by the sea.

We have been extremely lucky to have such a talented and devoted staff and group of consultants, and we feel even more fortunate that so many have been with us for so long. Particular thanks to Kevin Wolverton, Heidi Gordon, Myva Newman, Sotiris Kechris, Jean Dalton, and Jaxon Gwillim—stalwarts all—for their invaluable contributions to the firm over these many years. Connie Yu, Karen Momper, Leigha Delbusso, Evan Fraser, Ellie Brooks, Don Smith, Doug Woods, Nicky Kaplan, Anette Meertens, and Lauren Allen have been vital contributors to our work. We are also appreciative of so many who helped in countless ways: Kate Marshall, Shanta Pandit, Mark Przekop, David Williams, Helena Freeman, Amy Rosenstein, Trish Battistin, Karen Madrid, Rose Pardo, Scott Carty, Larkin Owens, Elizabeth Few, Jilana Stewart, John Bernatz, Tina Brand, and Alexis Moore-Jones. Our longtime trusted advisors (and friends) Karen Bodner and the late Michael Olecki kept us on course from the day we founded the firm. Architect Mark Woodley, interior designer Alysa Weinstein, and designer Linda Zelenko deserve our thanks for their contributions to the New York projects. We had the joy of working with the late great decorator Joe Nye on the Pasadena project. The many other talented designers whose work appears in this book are listed in the Sources.

The late Elizabeth Page contributed to our firm and to this endeavor in so many ways that are impossible to quantify or adequately express in words.

We are honored to have had such wonderful clients, many of whom we have worked with on multiple projects, in some cases over decades. It has been a joy to see so many of the houses and gardens we have designed grow up with the families that live in them and to have had the privilege of re-shaping them as the families' needs and visions have evolved. We are deeply grateful to these clients for the opportunities they have given us and for graciously allowing us to document their homes and gardens in this book.

From the very start, Jill Cohen was instrumental in clarifying the narrative of this book. Her ability to conceptualize the most effective way for stories to be told through the juxtaposition of images was both an education for us and a vital organizing principle for the book.

We were certain from the beginning of this project that we wanted authors who knew us well to write about our work. Fortunately, we happened to be acquainted with two of the best. The gratitude we owe to the inimitable Judith Nasatir is on the order of the National Debt. A brilliant, patient, tireless, and talented writer, Judith took all of our ramblings about these decades of work and turned them into elegant prose. We are also extremely grateful to Pilar Viladas for her deep insight, intelligence, and acumen in distilling our diffuse stories into a clear narrative for her much-appreciated Foreword.

Principal photographer Roger Davies, with whom we had the immense pleasure of collaborating on this project, has brought our work to life through his photographs. His unerring compositional eye and ability to look at our work in new ways have been inspiring.

It was also a delight to work with Francesco Lagnese, who photographed the two New York projects so beautifully. We are grateful to the other extremely talented photographers whose work is represented in this book, particularly Tim Street-Porter, whom we've had the pleasure and privilege of working with so many times over the years.

These beautiful photographs wouldn't be what they are without the assistance and vision of stylists Franco-Giacomo Carbone and Greg Bissonnette and the varied contributions of Jason Martin, Zoe Hennessey, Gemina Aboitiz, Jenessa Goodman, and Emily LaCoste.

This project has been a personal journey from the outset. It all began with the introduction by our good friends Cheryl and Ed Decter to our supportive, wonderful, and laser-sharp editor at Vendome Press, Jackie Decter. The enthusiasm, support, encouragement, and insights of Mark and Nina Magowan at Vendome Press, the fine work of book designer Patricia Fabricant, and the production expertise of Jim Spivey have made this challenging endeavor an extraordinary and rewarding experience.

271

PAGE 1: A driveway/entry court gate opens onto a secret kitchen garden near the back of a neo-Portuguese quinta perched on a hilltop overlooking the Pacific. **PAGES 2–3:** An eighteenth-century painted panel offers a formal welcome in the light-washed entry hall of a house for Francophiles in Rancho Santa Fe, California. **PAGES 4–5:** Outside the upper entry foyer of our renovated Harwell Hamilton Harris house, we reimagined a Japanese garden in the spirit of what might have been. **PAGES 6–7:** In the entry court of a property inspired by French and English precedents, a garden destination with seating offers an unexpected welcome into the layered landscape. **PAGES 8–9:** Looking out on the vastness of the Jackson Hole landscape, a double-height living room with a massive hearth mirrors its surroundings. **PAGE 10:** On our property, a carefully choreographed pathway provides a sense of procession from the house to the pool garden. **PAGE 11:** Potted kumquats infuse the transition between our house and pool area with scent and color. **PAGE 12:** Surrounded by torch aloe and agave, the lily pond in our pool house garden echoes the color motifs that help to weave the interior and exterior into a unified vision. **PAGE 270:** At a residence for Francophiles, Nicole de Vesian's drought-resistant gardens influenced our transformation of a kitchen courtyard area from a beautifully manicured lawn into an equally elegant but far less thirsty composition reminiscent of the south of France. **THIS PAGE:** Mac, Monkey's brother, always has the last word.

PHOTO CREDITS

All photos by Roger Davies, with the exception of the following:
Michel Arnaud: p. 168 bottom row center | Grey Crawford: pp. 199 top row center; 212 top; 224 top; 225 bottom right | Francesco Lagnese: pp. 200–11; 214–23 | Melba Levick: p. 138 center | Thomas Ploch: p. 83 top row center | Jeremy Samuelson: p. 138 top | Tim Street-Porter: pp. 57 bottom left; 83 center row right; 139 top right; 212 bottom; 213 bottom left; 265 bottom | Brian Tichenor: pp. 56 center row left; 57 top left and right, bottom right; 82 top and bottom; 83 top row left, bottom row left and right; 107 top row right, bottom row left, center, and right; 139 bottom left and right; 168 top row left, center row left and right, bottom row left; 169 top; 199 bottom right; 225 top left, bottom center; 264 center right | Dominique Vorillon: pp. 106 bottom; 225 center left

ARTIST CREDITS

All artists whose works appear in the photos are credited in the captions, with the exception of the following:
Karen Blair, portrait of Tina Brand, 2005: p. 213 bottom left | William Brice, *Untitled #6 Grey Field*: p. 28 (center) | Lorser Feitelson, *Magical Space Forms*, 1954–57: p. 72–73 (left) | Sir Godfrey Kneller, *Portrait of William III of Orange*: pp. 90–91 | Claudia Laub, print from *Loteria* series *La Artista*: pp. 44–45 (left) | Robert Lazzarini, portrait of Tina Brand: p. 212 bottom | Andrew Masullo, *5030*, 2008–10: p. 74 top (left) | John McLaughlin, *Untitled*, January 1954: p. 72–73 (right) | Farhad Moshiri, *Numbers*, 2004: p. 57 bottom left |Stephen Piscuskas, oil painting: p. 206 | Hovsep Pushman, *Redemption No. 601*, ca. 1950: p. 145 center right; *Coming of the Dawn, No. 420*, ca. 1940: p. 158 top left | Rembrandt van Rijn, etching: pp. 44–45 (top right) | Sara Lee Roberts, *The Avenue*: pp. 96–97 | Henri Sinclair, *Beaches in Deauville and Normandy*, early 20th century: pp. 256–57 | Pat Steir, *From the Boat: Constellation*, 2002: p. 176 | Brian Tichenor, encaustic painting: pp. 44–45 (bottom right); encaustic on panel (left), acrylic on panel (right): p. 53 top; encaustic on panel: p. 108; acrylic on panel: p. 116 | Emerson Woelffer, *Untitled (Chair Series)*, 1994: p. 74 top (right)

First published in the United States of America by
The Vendome Press
www.vendomepress.com
Vendome is a registered trademark of The Vendome Press, LLC

ISBN 978-0-86565-338-2

Editor: Jacqueline Decter
Production Director: Jim Spivey
Designer: Patricia Fabricant

Developed in conjunction with Jill Cohen Associates

Library of Congress Cataloging-in-Publication Data

Names: Tichenor, M. Brian, author. | Thorp, Raun, author. | Nasatir, Judith.
Title: Outside in : the gardens and houses of Tichenor & Thorp / M. Brian Tichenor and Raun Thorp with Judith Nasatir ; foreword by Pilar Viladas ; photography by Roger Davies.
Description: New York : Vendome Press, 2017.
Identifiers: LCCN 2017026167 | ISBN 9780865653382 (hardback)
Subjects: LCSH: Tichenor & Thorp (Firm) | Architecture, Domestic--Themes, motives. | Gardens, American. | BISAC: DESIGN / Interior Decorating. | ARCHITECTURE / Interior Design / General. | ARCHITECTURE / Buildings / Residential.
Classification: LCC NA737.T48 A35 2017 | DDC 728--dc23
LC record available at https://lccn.loc.gov/2017026167

This book was produced using acid-free paper, processed chlorine free, and printed with soy-based inks.

Printed in China by OGI
First printing